Why did you ̶ with the perso

Do you want to improve your relationship?

Do you want to save your marriage?

Have you ever wanted to pull away from someone who was hurting you, yet couldn't seem to end the relationship? Or have you ever avoided someone who was good to you because you didn't feel attracted to that person?

Have you ever wondered *why*?

If you are one of those many people who have made the same mistake again and again in relationships . . .

- ❤ *if you can't understand why you married the person you did*
- ❤ *if you find yourself saying the same things to your partner that you heard your parents say when you were a child*
- ❤ *if you hear your partner saying those same things to you now*
- ❤ *if you don't even know what mistake you are making*
- ❤ *if you're still wondering if any of this makes any sense at all*

. . . here's your chance to find out what's really going on. This book begins with an easy-to-take test that will help you understand exactly why you pick the mates you do—and what you can do about it!

Dedicated with love
to my mother and father
in the empty chairs

WHY WE PICK THE MATES WE DO

A STEP-BY-STEP

PROGRAM TO SELECT A BETTER PARTNER

OR IMPROVE THE RELATIONSHIP

YOU'RE ALREADY IN.

ANNE TEACHWORTH

$14.00 USA $17.00 IN CANADA

The descriptions of clients and situations in this book have been changed to protect their confidentiality. With the exception of the famous people referred to in some of the examples, the other examples no longer bear any resemblance to actual people, living or dead.

First Printing, 1997
Second Printing, Revised 1999

Printed in the United States of America

Library of Congress Catalog Card Number 97-093118

ISBN: 1-889968-53-6

Published by:
THE GESTALT INSTITUTE PRESS
The Gestalt Institute of New Orleans/New York, Inc.
1539 Metairie Road, Suite E
Metairie, Louisiana 70005 USA

1-800-GESTALT
http://www.Gestalt-Institute.com
e-mail: ateachw@aol.com

*Psychogenetics and The Selection Test are trademarks
of Gestalt Institute of New Orleans/New York/Inc.*

TABLE OF CONTENTS

III. THE ANSWER

IV. THE PATTERN

V. THE REASON

VI. THE HISTORY

VII. THE HOMEWORK

VIII. THE RESULTS

IX. THE SOLUTION 241

CHARTS & GUIDES

ACKNOWLEDGMENTS

For their support of this book along the way, my thanks to Emily Adams ❤ Jill Allen ❤ J.B. Anderson ❤ Sally Armel ❤ Robbie Bankston ❤ Tom Bernos ❤ Jim Bourne ❤ Jennifer Boles ❤ Norm Bray ❤ Vicki Butler ❤ Lynne Arnold Ciafre ❤ Cynthia Cousins ❤ Tom Devine ❤ Kay Duvernet ❤ Warren Duclos ❤ Leal Dugas ❤ Anne Farmer ❤ John Fischbach ❤ Lyn Fischbach ❤ Mike Fennelly ❤ Barbara Arnold Foster ❤ Sam Halperin ❤ Bettie Frisby ❤ Mildred Gabriel ❤ Morgan Goodlander ❤ Bill Haber ❤ Bobby Henderson ❤ Arthur Hyde ❤ Earnest James Jr. ❤ Judy Kopfler ❤ Cindy Kuhnau ❤ Rose Kuhnau ❤ Winifred Lahme ❤ Jim Leasure ❤ Kathy Lund ❤ Ruby Lyons ❤ Billy Marks ❤ Dee Martin ❤ Corby McCarthy ❤ Janice McDermott ❤ Beach McDaniel ❤ Maureen Metiva ❤   Mike Metz ❤ Thomas Morgan ❤ Debra A. Namias ❤ Renate Perls ❤ Hal Pluche ❤ Dottie Porter ❤ Lenny Ravich ❤ Fernando Regalado ❤ Liz Redmond ❤ David Richmond ❤ Russell Rocke ❤   Rose Sedita ❤ Adrienne Spencer ❤ Bill Teachworth ❤ Dan Teachworth ❤ Doug Teachworth ❤ Mike Teachworth ❤ Tom Teachworth ❤ Tina Thomas ❤ Kathryn Tracy ❤ Al Viguerie ❤ Evelyn Viguerie ❤ Brooks Warren ❤ Joseph Zinker.

For their help in the production of this book, my special thanks to Len Foley, Elaine Hughes, Jeff Teachworth, Glen Trinchard and especially Jean Trinchard.

A very special thanks to my teachers over the years, Richard Bandler, Jai, Leland Johnson, Mary Ann Merksamer Gallaway, Laura Perls and my parents, Eunice and Edward Schekeler.

GOD GRANT ME THE SERENITY
TO ACCEPT THE THINGS
I CANNOT CHANGE

THE COURAGE
TO CHANGE THE THINGS
I CAN

AND THE WISDOM
TO KNOW
THE DIFFERENCE.

—Reinhold Niebuhr

This book is about knowing the difference. . . .

INTRODUCTION

How did you pick your mate? Was it her looks? Was it his sense of humor? Was it his warmth, energy, and enthusiasm? Was it her friendly demeanor?

Most people are surprised when I tell them that the reason they think they selected their mates is very different from why they really did. In fact, why we choose anything, from an ice cream flavor to the person with whom we plan to spend the rest of our lives, is not a result of what we really want but of how we're subconsciously programmed to select or reject what we want.

Most of our preferences don't come from our conscious mind.

We believe in love at first sight, when actually most relationships begin as love at second sight. You'll be surprised to learn how your subconscious attraction mechanism truly works. You'll be amazed how quickly the Psychogenetic System described in this book will improve your relationship patterns—from selection to solution.

Why We Pick the Mates We Do is an interactive book that begins with an easy-to-take Selection Test that will give you, the reader, more insight into your real reasons for selecting your past, present, and/or future mates than you could discover from ten years of seminars, counseling, and contemporary how-to books . . . and the Selection Test takes only ten minutes.

For decades, popular books on the subject of finding a mate have reinforced the myth that singles can consciously search for the person they want to meet. Lonely readers have been encouraged to list qualities they most wanted in a mate and told to carry such lists around to local singles dances or supermarkets. The problem with these suggestions is that they don't work. Consistently, most people ignored what they said they wanted in a mate; instead, they have trusted their instincts and gone on to make the same mistakes over and over. Inadvertently, they stumbled headfirst into the compelling rush of falling in love. The "happily ever after" fantasies of the deepest self were activated. The new lovers pictured themselves feeling that way forever— until reality set in and the relationship didn't work out the way they had hoped. Until now we haven't known why!

If you've ever been wildly attracted to someone who wasn't good for you, in love with someone you didn't like, or unable to find the kind of person you always wanted to be with, you are one of the thousands of people who have already experienced a conflict between what the conscious mind wants and what the subconscious mind needs. (P.S.: Your subconscious mind is in charge of finding the perfect match for you!) "Even though I pick different partners," a recent divorcee mused, "I keep getting the same horrible results. Can the Selection Test tell me why the same thing keeps happening to me in my relationships?"

The answer is a resounding yes!

Do you want to meet the perfect mate for you? Do you want to improve your relationship with the mate you've already met? Do you want to get married again and live "happily ever after" this time? Taking the Selection Test included in this book and reading the following chapters will show you not only why you've been magnetically drawn to certain partners in the past, but also will help you change your attraction pattern in the future. You can learn to master your subconscious attraction mechanism and stop having dead-end relationships. You may have learned something from each, but sometimes hindsight isn't even 20–20.

Experience is a tough teacher in affairs of the heart.

You may never know what went wrong in each relationship. For years, singles and couples alike have been waiting for the magic formula to fall into their hands so they can have the relationships they most want. Here it is!

Why We Pick the Mates We Do is the result of my twenty years as a therapist, counseling and studying couples. During this time, I became increasingly convinced that the troubles most couples have after marriage are not just adjustment problems, but latent personality changes which only surfaced as their relationship journeyed from one stage to another. Some of the universal laments I heard every day about these stages were:

1) "He wasn't like this when we were just dating!"
2) "Everything was fine until we had sex."
3) "If I'd had any idea living with her would have been like this, I never would have moved in together!"
4) "We never should have gotten married, but it's too late now."
5) "Since we have children, it's even worse."

Truly, there is nothing so heartbreaking as having children with the wrong partner. Many a saddened client has asked me, "Isn't there some way to know before I get married how it will turn out after?" That is exactly what this book is about! In the following pages, you will learn how to break free from your faulty relationship compass of the past and redirect your attraction antenna to pick out subconscious signals that will steer you in the direction of happiness. You'll learn how to tune into your perfect mate and tune out the blaring discord that your compulsive relationship mind has produced for you in the past. You will find out how to change your pattern.

The Selection Test in the first part of this book is simple and fast. I've seen it work hundreds of times in my private sessions and workshops. It has helped countless individuals overcome the fear, anxiety, and endless frustration that have resulted from years of misery-creating choices. The Selection Test takes the guesswork out of the mating game by predicting what a relationship would be like with a potential partner before you even get involved with that person.

If you are already married, *Why We Pick the Mates We Do* will identify the hidden problems at the core of your relationship and show you how to correct them, so that you can easily achieve the future you always hoped for. This step-by-step guide to "happily ever after" is filled with examples I have collected from over a thousand case studies.

The Psychogenetic System is not theoretical or complex. It works predictably and reliably with any person or relationship. It has worked with teenagers and the elderly alike, and has proven itself time and time again as the most important key to making all successful life-mate choices. Hundreds of people have been able to reprogram their negative relationship patterns once they finally understand what was really going on inside themselves.

Now it's your turn to find out why *you* pick the mates *you* do . . . and what will happen after *you* marry!

The Selection Test that begins on the next page is designed to uncover your subconscious programming. Read the instructions for Step One, but do not read further ahead in this book until after you have completed the test.

The Psychogenetic System will be explained as you read this book.

THE SELECTION TEST

Step One: Instructions

1. There are three steps to the Selection Test. The Childhood History Chart is Step One. You are to fill in the blank spaces under each specific category. Do not stop, think, edit, or change your first responses. The best answers are the first words or phrases that come to mind when you read each instruction. All answers are totally right if they reflect the way you really felt as a child then.

2. You have ten minutes to complete all eight sections on Part One of the chart. It's as easy as one, two, three. The faster you fill in your answers, the more accurate the test results will be. Let's begin at the beginning— your beginning!

3. Turn the page to the chart and start at Step #1, describing yourself as a child from birth to ten years of age. List personality traits, behaviors, feelings about yourself, etc.

4. Do the same for Steps #2–5, describing each person in that role and then, at #6–8, listing how each pair felt about each other, what they did together, and how they communicated and interacted in your childhood. If a parent was absent, write that and describe whatever you did know as a child about that adult.

5. Put a plus (+) or minus (–) on top of each section (#1–#8), to describe your overall experience of that person or relationship as it was in your childhood.

6. Place a check mark by the parent that was your favorite adult (#2 or #3), and another by the parent that was your favorite parent (#4 or #5). Sometimes they may not be the same person. If neither parent was your favorite, delete this step.

7. *On your mark, get set, go . . . !*

2. Describe the looks, personality, and behavior of your mother (or female parent) as the adult person she was when you were a child (0-10 years old):

8. Describe parents' relationship with each other when you were a child (0-10 years old):

6. Mother-Child Relationship:

4. Describe mother as the parent she was when you were a child:

1. Describe yourself as the child you were (0-10 years of age):

Test™
History Chart

3. Describe the looks, personality, and behavior of your father (or male parent) as the adult person he was when you were a child (0-10 years old):

7. Father-Child Relationship:

5. Describe father as the parent he was when you were a child:

Accessing Childhood Memories

Now that you have completed Step One of the Selection Test, let me explain why you may have experienced some stress filling in your answers. First, any test is a stress, but having only ten minutes from start to finish is another one. Secondly, my requests for information about the people and relationships in your family-of-origin are designed to bring you back in memory to a time in your life when you were a child, a time that you may or may not remember very well—a time you may not want to remember at all. Besides, trying to write down a lot of information within such a short time is a stress in itself, and trying to remember past events that might have been unpleasant may have brought up some unhappy feelings for you.

Many of you who take this Selection Test have seriously tried to forget those unpleasant or stressful times in your childhood and were resistant to being asked to regress to those days. "Some things are better left forgotten," you may be saying to yourself. But "forgotten" means that the data has dropped out of your conscious memory and is now stored in your subconscious mind. Even if you had a happy childhood, most of it has already slipped from conscious memory into subconscious storage anyway. We must therefore access your subconscious mind to recover the necessary information about your childhood that we need for the background part of this test. **Psychogenetics is the study of subconscious relationship patterns and the Selection Test is the first step to uncovering those patterns.**

It may help you to find a point in time where you can begin to review your childhood. Almost everyone remembers something from first grade. You may have some memory of your first day at first grade, or kindergarten. That was probably the first time you left the world of the known and entered alone into the world of the unknown. All change is stressful. This one certainly was and may be remembered or avoided for that reason alone. For the first time you left your familiar family environment. **Awareness is usually dulled by repetition, but awakened by contrast.** That's why the first day at school is usually one of the points in time that allow most adults to reclaim many of their dimmed childhood memories—who they were as a child, who their parents were, what was going on at home after school, and what their lives were like before kindergarten or first grade. And what difference does all that make, you ask? It's all over and done with by now—or is it?

Step Two: Family-of-Origin Exercise

1. On the next page, describe how you experienced your family during your childhood, from birth to ten years of age. It is important that you write down as much as you can remember about what was going on in your family life then, especially during your earliest years.
2. List each member of your family and put a plus (+) or a minus (–) sign by each one to describe your experience of that family member then.
3. If this exercise brings up some difficult feelings for you to handle, please write them down alongside that person's name.
4. If you can remember specific examples, events or traumas that happened to those people or with them, write that in, too.
5. Include your age and the ages of those family members as you describe these events and that environment during that time in your life.

FAMILY-OF-ORIGIN EXERCISE

Step Three: On Second Glance

What you have recorded here in these first two steps of the Selection Test will make a lot more sense to you later in this book than it does now; and you will benefit greatly from the time you took to do a thorough job. Take a few more minutes to go back over the Selection Test and reread all your answers, giving yourself all the time you need now to elaborate and write down some examples from memory in each section. You can write them on the Selection Test itself or use a separate piece of paper if you need more room.

However, it is important that you do not change any of your initial responses on the test—simply elaborate by giving specific examples or adding new memories that come to mind. It is also important that you describe each person and relationship in your family-of-origin as you experienced them then, not as they are now. Jot down any additional words or phrases verbatim as you think of them.

Do not worry if your answers do not make sense, are not logical or chronologically accurate, or if you no longer think or feel that way about your parents or your relationships with them. Your parents may have changed dramatically since childhood.

You may be wondering if all this remembering and recalling is worth your time. Trust me, it is. You are already on your way to discovering more about your mating process than you ever thought possible. The information you have given about yourself will help you later with the evaluation of your relationship process.

However, not everybody who reads this book is ready to do the intense transformational work it invites you to do. You may indeed decide to read through the book first and then come back and do the written exercises separately. The questions at the end of some sections are designed to increase your awareness and make connections for you in your subconscious mind even if you do not consciously realize it or remember what happened in your early childhood.

NOTE:

If you do not want to write down your answers to the exercise questions on the following pages, simply read through the questions and pay attention to the first answers that come to mind.

Although writing is an important part of the self-discovery process, from this point on it is recommended but optional. The exercises and questions that follow will jog your subconscious mind whether you write them down or not.

The real voyage of discovery consists not in seeking new land, but in seeing with new eyes.

—*Marcel Proust*

I. THE QUESTION

We are the only culture that makes romance the basis of our marriage and love relationships and the cultural ideal of "true love."

—Robert Johnson

1. The Fairy Tale Begins

Once upon a time, as the storybooks say, the prince and princess met, fell in love, got married, and *lived happily ever after*. No mention was made in fairy tales of sex or children, only romance. In real life, however, things are somewhat different. Typically, today, two people meet, fall in love, have sex, live together, and get married, not necessarily in that order. Sometimes a couple gets pregnant. Sometimes they have the baby, sometimes they don't. Sometimes they get married because of the baby and sometimes they don't. Often they break up. Each progressive stage in a couple's relationship produces another set of hurdles for them to cross. Along the way, people fall in and out of love for reasons they do not understand. One out of every two couples who marry do not live happily ever after. They divorce.

As we approach the end of the twentieth century and enter the new millennium, our beliefs about marriage are rapidly changing. Like fine wine, tire treads, and light bulbs, marriage is one of those things in life where quality has traditionally been judged by longevity. In spite of its current track record, marriage *till death do us part* is still considered the ultimate achievement in couple relationships and what couples in love should strive for. It may surprise you to know, however, that only in the last few centuries have couples been marrying for love.

One of our most popular legends, Camelot, tells the

tale of Guinevere and Arthur, a marriage arranged for political reasons. As the story goes, Guinevere journeyed to Camelot to marry King Arthur, whom she had never met, and accidentally encountered him as she stopped to rest in the forest. Magically, they fell in love without her knowing he was the man to whom she was already pledged to marry. The best of all possible worlds, you say. Not so, as the story goes.

Marriages in those days were not based on romantic love. That was usually a separate component altogether. Romantic love was the emotional ecstasy one or both persons felt for the other that raised their earthly emotions to a spiritual level. Physical love was thought to be a lower energy. The sex act was primarily for the release of lust or the procreation of children. Marriages, therefore, were not love matches, but legal sexual contracts to protect children and property rights.

Before modern times, parents arranged or blocked unions of sons and daughters with little regard for the feelings of their offspring. Parents often literally gave daughters away in marriage to men they neither knew nor liked. In the case of Romeo and Juliet, the lack of parental consent to marry prevented their legal union but not their secret blessing by a cooperative priest. Their romance gave new meaning to the phrase *till death do us part.*

Romantic love was non-sexual and permitted between a married lady and the knight who worshiped her, carried her scarf, and slew dragons in her honor. A little exaggerated, perhaps, but you get the idea. But Gwen and Lance changed the game. As we all know, the Queen fell out of love with the King and in love with the knight in shining armor. In today's lingo, they had an affair. Their passion for each other was consummated in the physical act of sexual intercourse instead of expressed through ballad writing and adoration. Alas, Gwen cheated on Art and broke the marriage bond. But adultery did not result in divorce in those days. Marriage was *till death do us part.* The Queen went to a nunnery instead and the days of Camelot came to a tragic ending, as do many marriages today.

2. Marrying for Love

Despite these mythical warnings, the idea of needing romantic love in marriage has flourished. Over the centuries, falling in love has gradually become the primary reason for marriage. Although more and more couples began marrying for love, until the last generation parental consent remained important and a suitor was still expected to ask the girl's parents for her hand in marriage. Couples in love got married mainly to have sex and their marriage vows were for a lifetime. Of course, lifetimes were a lot shorter then than they are today.

Few couples two generations ago reached their twenty-fifth anniversary. Death parted most couples after about two decades and left many widowed. There were few divorces, and adultery was the only legitimate reason for the divorces that did happen. Sex *outside* marriage was frowned upon—before, during, and after.

Times have certainly changed again. Divorce, which was on the increase from the mid-sixties to the mid-eighties, has finally plateaued over the last decade. That drop in the divorce rate may, however, parallel the drop in the marriage rate. Having sex has become a part of the courtship process for people of all ages, and for many, living together has replaced the formal engagement period. Most young couples today marry to have children..

Unfortunately, as the joke goes, marriage is now the prime cause of divorce. Whereas the first sign of marital trouble was once called the Seven Year Itch, the average marriage today only lasts seven to eleven years.

QUESTIONS:

1. What does marriage mean to you?
2. If you are single, what are your reasons for wanting to get married? If you are already married, what were your reasons for getting married?
3. Are those reasons still important to you today, or have you other reasons for getting or staying married now?

3. The Search for Prince or Princess Charming

Is it marriage itself that is the problem, or our lengthened life span? Are we marrying for the wrong reasons? What are the right reasons? Are we marrying and divorcing too fast? Might our selection of partners be part of the problem? What do we find when we dig deeper than the historic attraction to "tall, dark, and handsome" or "five-foot-two, eyes of blue?" This book will give you a practical, easy method of improving your relationships from selection to solution.

Why do you pick the mates you do? By the end of this book, you will have more answers to that question than you ever believed possible. You may not like the answers you have gotten, but they will likely make more sense to you than any other theory you have believed or read about before.

Listen to what one of my clients, Jan, says. "Three years ago, when I decided I wanted to get married again, I was at a loss to understand why I never met the kind of man I would want to marry. The guys I liked were already married or they didn't like me. Only the men I wouldn't want to marry wanted to marry me. I had already passed up a dozen opportunities to get married, or shall we say, *avoided* a dozen. Three times I had actually gotten angry and ended the relationships before any chances of a real commitment emerged. I now understand why I have never gotten remarried even though I've always said I want to remarry. I now understand the conflict between what my conscious mind wants and what my subconscious mind needs. I had never even heard of Psychogenetics before I took the Selection Test. Now, because of it, I finally understand my own programming."

What is Psychogenetics, you ask? And programming?

Well, everyone has a subconscious map of the world. It's what guides you daily, minute to minute, person to person. **You may decide what you'd like to have in a mate, but there's an unrecognized, programmed part of you that decides whom you get, and you have little to say about its goal.** As you read this book, you are going to meet that part and understand yourself far better than you ever have before.

QUESTIONS:

1. What haven't you understood about yourself in relationships?
2. What still puzzles you about your parents' relationship?

4. For Better or Worse

We all know that marriage ruins some of the best relationships. Couples who have lived together happily for years as lovers get married and suddenly start having problems adjusting. These are not arranged marriages between strangers who do not know each other. Some even have a child already. Surely, you would think, they know each other well enough. What surprises could be left?

"I don't know what happened to us," the new bride says, sobbing as she tells me she has left her childhood sweetheart barely three months after their wedding day. "Everything was fine . . . until we got married, and then he was so different. I never dreamed he would treat me that badly. He turned into some kind of monster I'd never seen before."

Years ago, people would refer to this first adjustment difficulty a newly married couple experienced as the honeymoon wearing off. More problems were expected with the coming of their first child, and then not again until the Seven Year Itch, when the man typically would experience a sexual wanderlust. Times, they are a-changing. The latest studies show that for the first time in history more women than men are being unfaithful in the first decade of their marriages. One in every three women has extramarital sex in the first ten years, compared to one in every four men. The facts show that forty percent of all partners have at least one extramarital affair sometime during their marriage.

Undaunted by these startling facts, singles everywhere persistently search for the magical fairy tale they so desperately want to believe is still out there. Countless numbers of singles are continually enticed by the dream of married bliss, though the promise of living happily ever after mysteriously eludes most of them over and over again and the prospects of the odds changing are indeed more Grimm than the fairy tales. In desperation, frustration, or liberation, people are forming new customs and lifestyles to cope with the increasing life span and the decreasing marital span.

QUESTIONS:

1. How long did your parents date before they married?
2. Was it their first marriage? Second?
3. Did either parent stay single after the relationship with each other ended? How long?

5. *Single by Choice or by Chance*

In the 1990s, for the first time in modern history, singlehood has become a legitimate lifestyle choice. The social outcast labeling of *spinster, old maid*, and even *widow* has become a thing of the past. No derogatory terms ever shadowed the single male, who was always referred to simply as a bachelor, or more elegantly as an eligible bachelor, terms which still are in use today.

Whereas singlehood had once been considered more of a shame for the female than the male, the tables have turned. *Single woman* now conveys more status than *housewife*. Only the ticking of the biological clock has lured some of these career women to the altar. In ever increasing numbers, men who once feared being trapped into marriage are now seeking women who want to settle down and raise a family instead of build a career.

At present, more than half the adult American population is single and will stay that way. **Many singles have given up on picking a lifetime partner and instead practice simultaneous relationships, serial monogamy, or celibacy.**

Nevertheless, year after year, countless numbers of unattached people still hopefully seek out and practice the latest methods of finding a marriage partner. They read how-to books, go to seminars, therapists, fortune-tellers, psychics, astrologers, dating services, matchmakers, singles' bars and clubs, and church groups, only to end up with more of the same unhappy results.

Half of all first marriages end in divorce within the first ten years and only one in every four marriages that last longer are reported to be happy unions. Eighty percent of men remarry within three years of their first divorce, while only sixty percent of women thirty-five years or under remarry within three years.

Females reportedly take a longer time to pick a second partner and some do not remarry at all. Their second husband, more often than not, must assume the role of a live-in stepfather, while on the weekends, her ex's second wife gets the dreaded title of wicked stepmother. Fighting over the parenting of "yours, mine, and ours" children is reported to be the number one reason sixty percent of second marriages end in divorce.

Twenty-five percent of third marriages and a whopping seventy-five percent of fourth marriages also end in divorce. Perhaps the odds for the third marriage are better because by then most partners are just too tired, or too broke from the ever mounting cost of divorce and living separately, to try again. Some just give up the search for the perfect mate and settle for one-night stands or dating with the freedom to continue seeing other people.

As a therapist, over the years I have heard many the lonely cry of a divorced person who longs for another relationship but is afraid of getting hurt again. After several of their perfect choices turned into nightmare relationships, these traumatized veterans are now extremely reluctant to get reinvolved. "My last husband was my last husband. Never again," is the only vow some disillusioned ex's will make now. Not surprising.

But what is surprising to most people is the constantly warring couple who marry and, for some reason, settle down to enjoy a great husband-and-wife relationship. No one would have guessed these two were the real Just Perfect for Each Other Couple, not even the happy couple themselves. Unless, of course, they had first taken the Selection Test, which would have clearly shown ahead of time that their new relationship would actually improve with age.

6. Yes, Virginia, There Really Is a Selection Test

For some couples, marriage magically brings out the best in each partner. Why?

"I guess I was finally ready to settle down," a long-time bachelor said, trying to explain why he had changed his lifestyle virtually overnight to marry a young divorcee he had met only a few months earlier.

The divorcee, Virginia, a churchgoing twenty-six year old, already had two young sons from her first marriage. She and Greg had a baby girl. Surprisingly, Greg has become a stay-at-home, loving stepfather and first-time Dad at forty-four.

"I'm happier than I've ever been in my life," Greg tells his old drinking buddies.

Was it just good timing? Was Greg simply waiting until he found the right woman? Did he know exactly what he wanted all along?

We usually quickly understand when a man marries a much younger woman, but what prompted Virginia to marry a drinking man that much older than herself? How on earth did she know that Greg would be so very different after they married? Did she intuitively sense he could settle down even though she had known him for such a short time? Was she just lucky?

"Are you kidding?" Virginia said in reply. "I had a terrible first marriage. I wasn't taking any chances the second time. I took the Selection Test first and made Greg take it too. Then I could tell right away he would stop drinking and be a good husband and father for my boys. What a relief to know ahead of time! I didn't want to make another mistake."

Smart thinking! The Psychogenetic System allowed Virginia to foresee before she got too involved with Greg what sort of relationship they would have after she married him.

"Finally," Virginia exclaimed, "there is a way for people like me to know whether getting married will change us for better or for worse."

EXERCISE:

1. List relationships of yours where you or your partner went from worse to better.
2. List relationships where you or your partner went from better to worse.
3. Identify the stage in each relationship when the changes happened
   Meeting
   Dating
   Having Sex
   Living together
   Getting engaged
   Getting married
   Having children:
   1st, 2nd, 3rd, 4th, 5th, 6th, 7th, 8th
   Raising teenagers
   Getting separated
   Getting divorced
   Getting remarried
   Stepparenting
   Grandparenting

7. *From Bad to Worse*

How often have you heard someone say "I'll never get involved with someone like that again," and then watch as he or she goes ahead and does it anyhow?

I can hear it now: "For some reason that I can't understand, I'm always attracted to the same type of partner, the ones who aren't good for me. It doesn't make one bit of sense."

You may have even said that yourself, or this:

"But I can't seem to meet any other kind. No matter what I do, I keep getting involved with losers. What is wrong with me? Whose fault is it?"

Questions like these are rampant among people whose relationships have gone sour. Their inability to know what went wrong prompts them to blame their partner.

"It must be her fault," or "It's a mystery to me," or "Women walk all over you if you treat them too good," they'll say. Sadly, they don't understand why this is all too often true.

To date, no one has adequately explained why so many good guys and gals pick such obviously bad mates for themselves in the first place, or why some supposedly right relationship choices turn out wrong once the couple marries.

"That's exactly what I was afraid of doing again," Virginia said. "A person can't always tell at first how someone they meet will be in the long run."

For some couples, however, the approaching marital trouble *is* very obvious from the beginning. Their early dating interaction is negative. They argue. They fight. They break up. Everyone thinks it's for the best. But, against all good advice, they make up and get married. "Not a snowball's chance in hell of those two being happy together," everyone agrees, and most often they'll be right.

But sometimes, Mr. and Mrs. Wrong for Each Other make it work for the sake of the kids. Often they just learn to put up with each other. They never were friends and never will be. Others choose to lead lives of noisy desperation. Though their family life is one long battleground, they stay together.

Why?

EXERCISE:

1. Have you ever been attracted to, infatuated with, or involved with someone you didn't like or argued with most of the time?
2. What drew you to that person and kept you there?
3. List each example and how far the relationship went.

8. *Friends or Lovers*

Conversely, let's consider people who always got along well and have been good friends for years, but have never gotten romantically or sexually involved with each other. Their family and friends wished they could be more than friends, but they don't feel that way about each other, and can't figure out why not, especially when they like each other in so many other important ways.

"Cheryl and I are both single and lonely. We've been friends for a long time. Too bad, but we just don't have that magic spark between us. I want that spark. I wish I'd never crossed that line from friendship to trying to date her. I've felt rather awkward around her ever since. Our friends still want us to get married anyhow. But I want to feel that passion that I'm supposed to have. It's a doggone shame, too. I like her. Everything else is so perfect. It doesn't make any sense."

Well, why can't Jack feel that way about Cheryl? And what is *that way* anyhow?

For many people, it *is* a clear-cut choice between having a friend and a lover. Longtime friends very often purposefully choose *not* to cross the line and run the risk of ruining their friendship by having sex with each other. They know things will change between them after sex enters the picture; but, not certain whether the change will be positive or negative, they prefer instead to choose another partner for sex, often one they don't like as much or know as well.

Sadly, best friends who become lovers and then "happily marrieds" are the exception rather than the rule. Most couples started off as lovers, then became friends at a later stage of their relationship. They either work through their differences or learn to tolerate them. If they can't find a way to get along and don't want to break up, they come to therapy. Then it becomes my job to find out what went wrong and help them fix it.

EXERCISE:
1. Name five friends of each gender and list their personality and behavior traits, favorite activities, and interests.
2. Describe their looks.
3. Put plus (+) or minus (–) by each trait.
4. Put a check mark by traits and interests that you have in common with each of these ten friends and an x mark by your differences.
5. Which of these friends are you sexually attracted to?
6. Which of them are attracted to you?

9. Unhappily Ever After

"Where's the nice, loving girl I used to know?" John asks. "Paula was so sweet to me when we first met. We were friends for years but I swear I don't know who she is now. She wasn't anything like this before we got engaged. What's wrong with her? I sure wish I'd known she'd turn into such a nag. She must have a multiple personality or something. Maybe we shouldn't get married after all. I loved her so much but I don't feel 'that way' about her anymore. Why did she get so bossy from the moment we started planning the wedding?"

And what about Jack and Melissa, childhood sweethearts who separated barely months after their big wedding, presents still unopened, leaving friends and family in shock? No one can figure out what happened to them either, especially the dismayed couple themselves. Melissa can't explain the emotional turnaround she experienced after she married Jack: "Something just came over me. All the passion went out of me. I didn't like being married at all. I should have stayed single. I was so much in love with him before. Why didn't I feel that way anymore after we got married?"

And they're not the only ones whose relationship goes bad.

"I used to have a perfect marriage," Elle said. "My husband and I were great friends until we had the kids, and then he gradually started drinking and staying out late. He says I pay too much attention to the kids, but they're little and need me. He's got to grow up and stop being such a spoiled brat. Nothing I can say gets through to him anymore. He has no patience with the kids and they are afraid of him. He acts just like the drunken father he hated. Why did things turn out this way? For the life of me, I can't explain why he's so abusive now. He was so nice before I got pregnant.

Maybe it had been just too much of an adjustment for him to be a father." Consistently, I began to notice how many of my clients had reported these dramatic personality changes, not just in their partners, but in themselves, as they moved from one stage to the next in their relationships. Sometimes the progression improved their relationship, others it impaired.

10. Nothing in Common

Over the years, it became increasingly clear that most
of the troubled couples who came to me for counseling
were experiencing more than just adjustment difficulties, which is what I had been trained to expect as a
therapist. But what I saw surfacing was a multitude of
serious mismatches, or so I thought then. Either the
couples didn't have enough in common from the beginning or the deeper problems didn't show up until they
reached a later stage of their relationship.

To put it simply, many had fallen in love with the
wrong person if they were to have the kind of relationship they said they wanted. By the time they realized
the dilemma, it was too late to get out of the relationship easily without heartbreak or a sense of failure.
Unhappy couples were already too deeply involved with
each other to let go of their relationship.

Some were still hoping to recapture the good feelings
they had between them in the beginning and had since
lost. Some of them had already realized they no longer
acted in a way that matched what they had said they
wanted before they got married. Some were sad and disillusioned by sudden changes in behavior and already
feeling hopeless. "Well," these clients told me, "the fascination has worn off," or "Our differences are too great to
reconcile."

Even with the popularity of therapy in the nineties, it
was already common knowledge in my profession that
traditional couple counseling methods took too long,
cost too much, and rarely brought successful, long-
lasting results. Like most therapists, I had often encouraged couples to argue it out or lectured them about
what they should be doing with each other—things they
wouldn't, couldn't, or didn't change. Couple counseling
was a rather new specialty then, only a few decades old

and still not well defined. Typically, in working with couples, I'd usually begin individual therapy with one or both partners and then move to teaching them better communication skills with each other.

The traditional therapeutic approaches I had been using required that my clients first resolve their own unfinished issues in their relationships with their parents (#6 and #7 on the Childhood History Chart). Couple sessions continued until each client's Inner Child (#1) realized that these unmet childhood needs could not be transferred as expectations into adult relationships. It was important that each client understand their parents as the adult human beings they were *then* and accept that these two people did not, could not, or would not meet their childhood needs *ever*.

It was also important that both mates learn to see their parents as the adults they were then, not as they could be, should be, or would be. We therapists believed that giving up one's need for the parents to change and accepting one's mate unconditionally would produce a loving adult relationship for both partners. Sometimes the couples could do it, sometimes they couldn't. Sometimes it worked, but too often it didn't. Giving up on that need for the partner to change often resulted in the couple giving up on their relationship altogether.

To make matters worse, I began to realize that the established counseling techniques I had been using might not have uncovered the real underlying issues that were causing the couple's difficulties in the first place. Improved communication skills helped temporarily but rarely fixed the imbedded problems which, to date, might never have been correctly identified.

It was time to do some of my own investigations in that direction. I wanted to see if I could come up with a practical way of quickly getting to a troubled couple's underlying problems. It was also my goal to develop some simple guidelines and exercises for unhappily married couples who really wanted to save their failing marriages.

I also wanted to improve my single clients' selection patterns before they got into relationship trouble with someone who was wrong for them. My hope was to develop a simple way for people to predict what the chances of a successful relationship would be with a certain partner *before* they had to find out the hard way. Hence this book began. . . .

II. THE RESEARCH

*Finding and keeping love is not just a romantic
idea. It's crucial to our intact survival.*
                                    —Harville Hendrix

1. Perfect Mate or Perfect Match

Five years ago in one of my Relationship Workshops,
I asked the clients who were present to each pick a
partner for the day. About thirty people had been
together for about twenty minutes prior to those
instructions, so the data they had on each other was
limited to names, voice quality, appearance, dress, body
language, and what little information had been shared
during the introductions. No one had any prior knowledge of the other participants' backgrounds, except me.

The opening exercise involved having them mingle
without talking, then pair off and sit next to each other.
I remember my amazement as I surveyed the participants as they sat down in pairs. One woman in particular stands out in my mind when I think back to then, for
it was in that moment the premise for this book was
born.

A new client, Elizabeth, had come to the workshop to
explore her repeated failures in relationships. As an
abused wife, still recovering from the latest of her three
bad marriages, she was highly reluctant to involve
herself in yet another hurtful relationship. To heal,
Elizabeth had remained isolated for the past two years.
However, as instructed, and without talking at all to
anyone in the room, she picked Ted for her partner.
After her long, careful deliberation, I had wondered if
she would pick anyone. Ted, sensing her hesitancy,

made his way over to her, too. It was a mutual attraction, love at first sight. Elizabeth sat next to Ted, appearing quite happy with her catch.

An attractive, clean-cut man in his early forties, Ted was tall and well built, casually dressed, and somewhat dignified. Only I knew he was "out of uniform." How had Elizabeth, the child of a stern Army captain father whom she had feared and hated, managed to select the only military man in the room? I asked myself.

Little did she know that Ted's ex-wife had left him barely a year earlier because of his temper. Ted was in therapy to work through his anger at women. He, too, had an abusive parent, only his was his mother. My initial assessment of Ted was that he had transferred his mother-child relationship with his mother onto both of his previous wives. Determined not to do it again, Ted, like Elizabeth, had avoided relationships since his divorce. Coincidence, you might say, as I might have also, had it not been for the number of equally coincidental pairings.

What had happened here?

2. Made for Each Other

This was a workshop filled with my clients, all of whom I knew exceedingly well and none of whom knew each other at all half an hour before. Nevertheless, with practically no sharing of background, the workshop participants consistently gravitated to the same type of person with whom they had had trouble in their previous relationships.

So here, as in life, they were about to get involved with people just like those they had sworn off. Only they didn't know it yet. They were in the process of finding it out. By midmorning, without even knowing they had similar histories, Elizabeth and Ted were already at odds and no longer happy about having chosen to be with each other for the two days of this workshop. Their selection of a particular mate was leading them right back into the same frying pan.

Perhaps, I thought to myself, this workshop would teach them how to interact differently and bypass the troubled areas of their past relationships. Possibly they could learn enough to give themselves some tools to take into their lives and change their unsatisfactory interactional patterns.

Optimistic? Yes. Realistic? No. Indeed, they did learn how to talk about their feelings with their workshop partners a lot more effectively and recognized some of the dilemmas that had plagued them with past partners. But it was I who was to learn more from this workshop than I could ever have imagined.

What was most enlightening for me was that I recognized the automatic interactional pattern repetition that each pair fell into as the workshop progressed. Left to their own resources for a few hours, they were back swimming in the same old shark-infested waters of flawed relationships, and in need of counseling to keep from drowning or getting eaten alive—not only Elizabeth and Ted, but most of the other pairs, too.

They had recreated their real life in the group. Some couples started as friends, happy to be with each other. Others seemed genuinely attracted to and excited by the other. A few were somewhat disgruntled that they hadn't been picked by the partner they originally wanted.

Later that afternoon, dissatisfaction with their choices surfaced and the participants began to compare their selection process in the workshop to their selection process outside the room. Some realized the similarity to their past relationships and were able to articulate their long-withheld feelings for the first time. Others just grieved. We did quite a bit of roleplaying of parent-child relationships and expressed a lot of suppressed emotion. Most of the participants said they had gotten more out of this experience than from any other workshop they had ever attended on couple relationships.

Even Elizabeth and Ted were able to work through the familiar conflict they had encountered during the workshop and parted friends. Both of them thought that was a small miracle, considering the amount of real life hostility and pain each had brought to their workshop relationship.

I left thinking the workshop had been a smashing success, yet wondering why they had said goodbye without any indication that they hoped to stay in touch afterwards.

QUESTIONS:

1. Have you stayed friends or enemies with past lovers or ex-mates? Or lost contact with them?
2. Have you stayed in an unhappy relationship or argued continually with a relationship partner?

3. After the Ball Was Over

As the months wore on, I began to notice that the clients who had attended that workshop were again making the same mistakes in their mate choices and getting stuck in the same places in their relationships, even though they now knew better. Why, after all they had learned there? I asked myself. Had they somehow forgotten? The question was the beginning of my search for the answer to *Why We Pick the Mates We Do*.

Several months later, I scheduled two more workshops in rapid succession with more clients who were new to each other. The same pairing phenomena happened there as in the first workshop, though I had asked this second group of participants to pair up after only ten minutes of an opening round. This time they had shared only their first names and not their reasons for being in this relationship workshop. That introductory round gave them half the time and much less information than in the first workshop. Inaccurately, I predicted that less time prior to pairing would lessen the coincidental repetitions of failed relationship choices. It increased them.

What happened at the second workshop prompted me to rethink my entire approach to counseling. The pairs that formed in the third workshop were even more mystifying for their coincidences. Within three minutes, with no preliminary name or data introduction at all, the increased coincidences of repetitive choice in the couple pairings amazed me. Clients who had been abused as children somehow found each other, and as the day wore on, these individuals seemed to be jockeying to become either victim or persecutor—depending on their usual role in previous relationships. Clients who did not have an abusive background, but who had been physically or emotionally abandoned and were eager to achieve closeness with a partner, stayed some-what distant from each other no matter how hard they tried to form lasting bonds.

A few couples managed to break through with self-disclosure and became overjoyed with their new-found intimacy. At the end of the first day, I gave all the unhappy pairs an opportunity to get couple counseling in the workshop, work it out themselves, or ask for a "divorce." When given this opportunity at the end of the first day, most of the distant couples were ready to start over again with someone new, while the abusive-back-ground pairs stayed together and seemed locked into resolving their issues.

All of these participants had only met the day before. Their bonding patterns intrigued me. Was it simply unfinished business from this relationship that they wanted to settle, or was this repetitive trouble coming from previous unsettled relationships? Was this trans-ference coming from their parent-child relationships as the popular theories said? I was determined to find out.

QUESTIONS:

1. Have you had the same problem or pattern in each of your past relationships?
2. Has the problem ever been settled?
3. Did you stay in the relationship anyhow? How long?
4. Did you have the same problem in childhood with a parent?
5. Did your parents have the same problem with each other?

4. Were They in a Bond or a Bind?

Transference is a highly predictable phenomena and one that psychotherapists see every day. What it means is that each person we meet reminds us in some small or large degree of some earlier person in our life, and, in the case of mates, usually one of our parents. For a while now, the most popular theory among psychologists has been that our mates are picked by our Inner Child and reflect our unmet childhood needs—needs not satisfied by our parents. Psychotherapists believed that counseling could bring about conscious awareness of these feelings, and that this in turn would stop the projection of these childhood expectations onto the client's partner.

Projection means that the same feelings and behaviors that originated in an earlier scene are now being attributed to a current situation; therefore, the automatic expectation is that this new person is similar to the earlier one, and this new person's automatic response will be the same as those of the person in the past.

Transference is a familiar cycle, even though it may not be a comfortable one. But given that the fear of the unknown is a basic human motivation, the uncomfortable known becomes a somewhat secure condition compared to its alternative—the unknown. In unhappy relationships, most people will want the other person to do something different first. Because of their fear of the unknown, both partners will resist changing their own behavior and continue to do the well-known thing, whether it works or not.

With few exceptions, the familiar set of cues and responses that couples rely on in those situations are usually traceable straight back to their family-of-origin, and so is their so-called solution. Consistently, most people are more interested in getting the other person to change, rather than looking at their own behavior. In a nutshell, that's usually why their interaction faltered and why they came to a therapist—to fix their partner!

QUESTIONS:
1. What did your mother want to change about your father as a mate?
2. What did your father want to change about your mother as a mate?
3. What did you want to change about your mother? Did she change it?
4. What did you want to change about your father? Did he change it?

5. Sex Changes Everything

"As long as we're talking about change," Gail asked me, "can your little Selection Test tell me why men are so different after you have sex with them? My boyfriend used to be so attentive before we made love. I wasn't ready for the way he is now. It's as if I'm with a total stranger. Something has gone out of our relationship and I can't figure it out. It's not the first time this has happened to me either. Having sex has ruined my relationships before."

"Guys change after you have sex with them," **Linda agreed, voicing one of the most typical** **complaints of females who are dating. Sheila** **voiced the other. "There just aren't any nice guys** **out there anymore."**

"Well, I'm a nice guy," Earl said. We were sitting in a weekly therapy group when Earl spoke up. "Somebody please tell me why nice guys finish last!" He had just learned that his new relationship with Carol was over. It was the second time he'd been dumped for an old boyfriend. "I swear both of these guys are jerks. Why do gals fall for guys like that who love them and leave them?"

It was a real good question. Books have been written about men who hate women and the so-called smart women who regularly make these foolish choices.

"Do I have to mistreat women to hold their attention?" Earl asked.

The fact is that there are a significant number of women who, year after year, become battered wives. Most of them have been abused as children, but for some reason, they repeatedly pick angry men. Equally shocking is the frequency with which men and women who are children of alcoholics either marry an alcoholic partner, or become one after they marry. Not to mention the men and women who become abusers or alcoholics, even though they left home to get away from an abusive or alcoholic parent. Somehow, despite all our efforts at recovery and counseling, the cycles of abuse and alcoholism in families continue to reappear and repeat themselves, unchecked and unexplained.

"Why did Louis fall in love with someone who mistreated him from the very beginning?" asked Meg, a pretty redhead from an Irish family of eight children. Last month she was shocked to find out that her nice-guy boyfriend of five years had just eloped with Ina, whom he met at college. "Louis hardly even knew her. They don't have anything in common. He even tells me that he doesn't know why he married her," Meg said, raising yet another point worth investigating.

How could her supposedly sensible boyfriend overlook the warning signs of approaching marital trouble that were evident to everyone else from the beginning of his tumultuous new relationship with this girl? Was it passion that clouded Louis's otherwise logical personality? Or rebellion?

"Both our mothers are brokenhearted about this, too. His mother wanted me to be her daughter-in-law. We get along better than she does with her own daughter," Meg cried.

"I'm sure Ina will settle down after we're married awhile," Louis had told Meg, but she didn't buy it.

"Ina's given him nothing but trouble from the minute he met her. I, on the other hand, did everything I could to make him happy for years. Now he wants us to stay friends. Why did he leave me for her? Couldn't he see how much I loved him? What makes him think she'll change?"

I wondered as I listened to her story, Is love that blind? Or simply naive?

"Well, it certainly was blind and deaf, too, in my case," Patrick added. "If I'd had any inkling of what I was getting myself into when I married Christy, I surely wouldn't have done it."

Well, it seems, if not blind or naive, love is either extremely near- or farsighted. Love often ignores facts in the present and concentrates on its fantasies for the future. People in love characteristically do not see the beloved's faults right under their noses. Universally, they prefer to think any differences they see will go away or can be worked out after they marry. **It does seem that a person in love is usually blind to the loved one's faults before they marry, and blind to their own faults afterwards.**

It's a paradox—how can we say love is blind and still believe in love at first sight? What is it that we are really looking for in a mate anyhow?

EXERCISE:
1. List the top ten traits you want in a mate.
2. List the traits you usually get in a partner.

6. *Love at First Sight*

According to Princess Caroline, her mother and father, Princess Grace and Prince Rainier of Monaco, met and fell in love at first sight. Within three days, they decided to get married. By all accounts, the union was much like a fairy tale. Princess Caroline took ten days to decide to marry after she met her first husband-to-be and said it was love at first sight for her, too. Love was not blind here. Both marriages were happy till death do us part.

I decided to take a second look at love at first sight. What does that phenomenon really mean anyhow?

TV talk show hosts George Hamilton and Alana Stewart talked about being happily divorced after being unhappily married. George said they got along well before they were married and even better after they divorced.

"Before we married," he said, "Alana was a very independent woman. I liked that. She always wanted to go out to fascinating places. But once we got married, she turned into Little Miss Homemaker and wanted to stay home. I didn't. She was always doing interesting things before we married. Now she's back to being interesting again. We saved our relationship by getting a divorce. We're great friends now. We were very adult about it."

That statement raised some very interesting areas to explore.

Featured on one of their TV talk shows was a private investigator who specialized in tracing people. He had been asked to trace Alana's father for the show. Separated from her father since she was fourteen months old, as a little girl Alana had written letters to him. It's important to state that Alana never saw her father after her mother moved out of town with her. The investigator produced the first information Alana had about her father in many years and brought her step-brother to meet her.

On the show, her new-found stepbrother brought Alana the sad news that her father had died, but told Alana about her father's life after her mother left him. The stepbrother also brought her one of the letters Alana had written her father when she was eight years old and showed her a picture her father had kept in his wallet until his death. It was a picture of her father holding Alana as an infant.

The resemblance between Alana's father and George Hamilton amazed me. I wondered if Alana had noticed it. Did George remind her of the father she had loved and lost a long time ago? Was their resemblance just a coincidence? Or had the memory of Alana's young father's face remained imprinted in her mind's eye since infancy? Indeed, was it love at second sight? Had Alana simply fallen back in love with a man who reminded her of her first love? Was it George's familiar looks, or perhaps something more than looks?

The beginnings of a new theory were coming together for me.

QUESTIONS:
1. Does your mate resemble either of your parents?
2. Or how one of your parents looked when you were a child?
3. Does your mate resemble you or one of your siblings in adulthood?
4. Do you look like one of your current mate's parents when he or she was a child?
5. Does your current mate remind you of either of your parents in other ways?
6. Does your mate's voice or accent remind you of one of your parents?

7. *Freudian Slip-Ups*

When I was a teenager, my mother told me that if I wanted to know what my boyfriend would be like when he got older, I should look at his father. My mother, like most people, unknowingly agreed with Freud's theory that a boy grew up to be like his father and a girl like her mother. We took Freud literally but transposed *be like* with *look like*.

Had Alana picked a husband who only looked like her father, or was George also like him in other ways? Very often, the mate does resemble one of the parents, but that is not the most determining factor in attraction. There's more to chemistry than good looks or physical likeness to one of the parents. Similar personalities seemed to play a large part. I began to study selection patterns by asking clients what they believed about picking the perfect mate, and what the outcome had been for them.

At twenty-six years of age, Lisa had just gotten divorced. She was glad to talk about her selection process. "As a kid, my mother was my favorite parent by far. I hated my father. I didn't want to marry a man anything like him. When I met my boyfriend's father, I liked him from the beginning. Peter's father liked me, too," Lisa told me. She described her father-in-law as intelligent, well read, with a loving nature.

"I married Peter, Jr., because I wanted to end up with a husband like his father, but I didn't. What a disappointment! My boyfriend looked like his father but he wasn't like him at all after we married. As a husband, Peter, Jr., behaved more like *my* father than like his. Both my husband and my father always have something bad to say about everyone. I used to call my husband Henry, Jr., after my father, because he was so much like him."

Maybe, I thought as I talked to Lisa, she would have been wiser to look at her own father first to see how her boyfriend would turn out after they married. After all, wasn't Lisa's father, Henry, Sr., the first male in Lisa's life? Her father would certainly be a true case of love at first sight for her as an infant, wouldn't he? Even if Lisa's father's personality had not been lovable later on, wouldn't that experience of being with her father as an infant remain in her feeling memory, too, not just in her mind's eye—or were they the same? I'd already asked myself that question over and over again. But here was a new question emerging. Why didn't Lisa, the adult, pick a man who could give her what she had wanted from her father in the first place, instead of a man who couldn't?

I got curious about the number of people I saw who, like Lisa, started off thrilled with a mate and then got to some point in the relationship where that changed for them. Some had ended their relationship right away, others at later stages. What had happened? Had they let looks from either the past or the present lead them astray? All too often they couldn't talk about it. Often after the breakup, oblivious to their own participation in the outcome, they blamed each other.

Many relationship problems began when one partner tried to change the other to match his or her own idea of how that partner should be. Where had that idea come from? The love that was blind to the other's faults at first sight saw those faults glaringly in hindsight. Hadn't they seen those traits at the attraction stage? Couldn't they see which qualities were missing from the beginning?

If we know love is blind, how come we believe in love at first sight? Aren't those two beliefs in conflict with each other? Had their heart or their passion over-whelmed their better judgment? Was it just all memory from childhood? Was it really the Inner Child part of the personality that chose a partner in adulthood?

I began investigating that angle.

EXERCISE:

1. Turn back to #2 and #3 of the Selection Test. Which of your parents was your favorite adult when you were a child?
2. What did you particularly like about that parent?
3. Do you have any of those qualities in yourself now, or do you see them more in your partner?
4. Which of your partner's parents is your favorite?
5. Does that person have any of those qualities?

8. *The Inner Child*

Most people have heard about the Inner Child, that part of our personality that represents all our childhood feelings and experiences. Most of the theories on mate selection and relationship counseling state that the difficulties a person experiences with an adult mate are a direct result of the Inner Child's unmet needs with one of the parents. **"Unmet needs" refers to the legitimate emotional or physical dependency needs which were never met in childhood by a parent whose job it was to meet them.**

Inner Child work is a most effective way to help the average adult resolve some of his or her unmet needs. More and more we are finding that these unmet needs are the ones our conscious mind didn't or couldn't deal with as a child. We couldn't resolve them then and the adults in our childhood family couldn't either. Often these traumatic experiences from childhood had to be kept secret for one reason or another. In effect, they were kept so secret that the child forgot them as he or she grew up. They remained hidden in the subconscious memory as repressed feelings. Stored deep inside the subconscious mind, it's not until the Inner Child grows up that these feelings are either automatically repeated in adult relationships or avoided like the plague.

Couple therapy has historically been based on the belief that your childhood unmet needs are now being projected onto your current relationships and are causing unrealistic expectations that your partner cannot fulfill. Therapists usually work with clients to get them to realize that meeting these needs was the job of their parents, not their mates. Those who believe in the parent-child unmet needs theory say that the Inner Child picked a partner to meet the same needs that weren't met by a parent in childhood.

Our early memory base has recorded the good, the bad, and the ugly feelings. What happened to and around us was imprinted in the subconscious mind. The more unpleasant the memories, the more the conscious tendency to forget the whole thing. Forgetting simply means not being able to recall those things. The feelings associated with the event were buried inside, but, unfortunately, they were buried alive. Feelings that are buried alive control our behavior without ever letting our conscious mind know why we are doing or not doing some things. They rob us of any choice in the matter. We just react. **They now control our behavior as adults, without our knowing it. It is important that we find these repressed programs to deactivate them.**

QUESTIONS:

1. Did you have any traumas, abuse, death, accidents, divorce, or abandonment in your early childhood? At what age?
2. Did your parents? Either in their childhood or during yours?
3. Do you remember these events or were you told of them?
4. Does your current partner have any of these same events in his or her family-of-origin? What about any former partners?

9. Picking From The Head

Popular books on the subject of finding a mate have too long reinforced the belief that singles can consciously search for the mate they want. Lonely readers have been encouraged to make handy reference lists of positive qualities desired in a future mate and to keep said lists in their pockets or purses for handy reference at singles dances, parties, bars, or supermarkets. But repeatedly, most of us, when faced with an attractive new prospect, ignored what we said we wanted and proceeded to fall head over heels in love and make the same mistake in selection repeatedly.

Why are we so helpless to choose or change?

Fortune tellers say it's fate that brings a couple together. Metaphysicians say it is a supersoul choice before birth. Song writers say it is the moon and the stars that bring lovers together. Astrologers say it is the Sun and Moon, or Venus and Mars. In his number one bestseller *Men Are From Mars, Women Are From Venus*, John Gray says it is advanced communication skills that bring the two genders together. Perfume makers believe it's pheromones. Researchers believe it's hormones.

A friend of mine said she couldn't even get attracted to anyone lately. "I probably need hormone shots," Amber said. Hormones or pheromones? She made me wonder about the chemistry that makes us select or reject a lover. Desmond Morris says it's smiles, bright colors, and grooming gestures. Toothpaste makers say it's all in having sparkling pearly whites. Old wives say, "The way to a man's heart is through his stomach." New wives say, "It's through his penis."

A client named Ron said he's always attracted to women who are good cooks, but after a few weeks he doesn't feel real sexual with them anymore. Instead, he feels like he's at home with his mother. We used to say that a man like Ron had a Madonna/Whore Complex. "But that was before Madonna came along and blurred the two terms for me," Ron quipped, laughing off the number of relationships that never worked out for him. "I'm just not turned on anymore either way."

What are the mysterious ties that either bond or bind? What is the chemistry that attracts two people to each other? What is the magic that makes two people want to spend the rest of their lives together? And what is the reason some of them last and some of them don't? Why do people change so much after they live together or marry?

Sigmund Freud said that we marry a person like our parent of the opposite sex and take on the role of our same-sex parent. I wasn't so sure of that anymore. His theory was role- and gender-bound: Basically, girls want to marry their fathers and boys want to marry their mother.

"Maybe that was true for me in childhood. But not now for heaven's sake," Amber sighed. "I know I'm still waiting for my prince to come but I can guarantee he won't be anything like my father, or my step father, when he does. Each time I meet a new guy, I think he's the perfect mate for me. But, of course, it doesn't turn out that way. They don't act right or do what they're supposed to do. When he even starts to remind me of my lazy, good-for-nothing father, I get aggravated and leave. Sometimes I stick around for a few days or weeks, but lately, it's gotten to be till *dawn* do we part.

"My mother tells me I'm just too picky, but look where not being picky got *her*. She tells me not to make the same mistakes she did. But I'm not the least bit interested in marrying someone like my father. In fact, I'm avoiding doing that. I want someone exactly the opposite of him."

10. Picking from the Subconscious

After Freud came Carl Jung. Jungian Theory says a woman has her anima (female traits) more conscious in her personality and her animus (male traits) in her subconscious. A man has his animus traits (male traits) more conscious in his personality and his anima (female traits) in his subconscious. Jung said each of us has the other gender in our subconscious and will pick a mate that has the other side of our traits.

Carl Jung believed that a man seeks to marry a woman who matches his inner feminine side (anima) and a woman seeks to marry a man who matches her inner masculine side (animus). Jung said we seek our opposite, or shadow, for completion and wholeness. The anima and animus are not gender bound. Jung stated that he was referring to feminine and masculine personality traits and not physical gender roles. His theories were spirit bound. Now there was an interesting new angle to explore, personality.

Listen to Peggy's story: "I love Larry but I just can't stand being around him anymore." After three months of living together, Peggy had moved out and was coming to me for counseling. "I fell in love with Larry right away. He was so charming when we met. But this is another side of him. Larry has something bad to say about everything I do now. He's always on my case about something. He's turned into a real grouch. The only other person I know like that is my mother. She's always mad at the world and unhappy. My mother found something wrong with everybody. I love her, but I can't be around her either.

"When I met Larry I wanted to get away from my mother. Larry looks a lot like my father, but isn't at all like him. My father is a very happy person. He's my favorite parent. Daddy leaves the room when my mother starts ranting and raving because she makes him so unhappy. I don't want a relationship like my parents have had. I had enough of that a long time ago. How did I go and get right back in it? I never would have thought he'd be like my mother. No wonder I hate Larry now."

EXERCISE:

1. Given the way you described each of your parents as adults on the Childhood History Chart in Step One of the Selection Test (#2 and #3), which of your parents is your current (or latest) partner most like?

2. Write your partner's name on top of this parent's Adult section of the chart. This parent was your Mate Model and your current (or latest) partner who is most like this parent is called your Inner Mate.

3. Now place your name on the other parent's Adult section of the Childhood History Chart. Let's call that parent your Adult Role Model, and you the Inner Adult partner.

III. THE ANSWER

The people who are attracted to you are attracted to you not by what you do or who you are, but by what you think.

—Napoleon Hill

1. Why Do You Speak English?

That is the question I have asked my clients after they have just completed the Selection Test about their childhood. The question is designed to get you to stop and think about the impact of cultural and environmental surroundings on you as a young infant. The answer, of course, is that as a child, you spoke English because you grew up in a family with English-speaking parents and you learned it by listening to what was repeated around you. We could say you were conditioned to speak English. It's your native tongue because it's the first language you heard and you learned it because, as an infant, the people around you spoke English all the time. They whispered to you in English. They told secrets to each other in English and shared their most intimate conversations in your presence. You were just a baby to them and not able to understand English—or so they thought, merely because you couldn't yet speak it.

Your parents talked and interacted in front of you every day of your childhood without realizing that every word, every action, and every behavior of theirs was being recorded in your subconscious mind and had been from the time of your birth. They never taught you English grammar, accent, tone, or sentence construction. You, as an infant, absorbed it by listening to your family-of-origin. You weren't taught it; you caught it, or rather caught onto it. So much so that by the time you were two years of age, you had begun to speak English yourself.

At two years of age, you had already comprehended one of the most difficult-to-master languages in the world. How did that happen? By conditioning, or shall we say, by hypnosis. Most people speak exactly like their family, and like it or not, their voices sound particularly like their gender role model. Even if they don't recognize the similarity, everyone else does. We all have had the experience of being taken for someone else in our family over the phone. The tonality and inflections of the adults around us were thoroughly absorbed before we were two years old, as was their set of cues and responses. We were programmed to talk like our family.

"Oh, he's just a baby. He doesn't understand what you're saying," adults say in front of an infant. Yet, by the time that infant is barely a few months old, he or she has begun to respond not only to the sound of familiar voices, but to specific words and phrases. The infant brain has already begun to process experiences and link them to particular sounds and patterns of words that are part of the environment we call our family-of-origin. Those familiar sounds become the infant's native tongue.

Within their first two years, everyone learns to speak in their parent's language. Your parents didn't teach you sentence construction. That would be perfected later. The extent of early language training an infant usually gets is limited to "Momma," "Dada," "Nana," or "baby," "ball," "bottle," and "Bubba." No matter how good one's early memory is, no one remembers being taught English. You learned it by repeatedly interacting with your environment. **Repetition produces conditioning and conditioning is programming.**

Almost by osmosis, the infant begins to understand how to interact with the familiar environment in the same tones, volumes, and sounds with which the environment interacts with him or her. You learned not just what to say, but when, how, and to whom. The impact the early environment has upon each infant is permanent and lasting whether it is consciously remembered or not.

EXERCISE:
1. List five belief systems and values you share with your mother.
2. List five belief systems and values you share with your father.
3. How many do both agree on?
4. What were their conflicts about?

2. Doing What Comes Naturally

By the time you are five years old, certain verbal cues and responses have already been established between parent and infant, and between others in the home. Interactional patterns that are present in the early life of the infant and toddler are said to be imprinted, much the same way as the absorption of the natural language is imprinted. What this book is about, is the imprinted adult-adult and parent-parent relationship patterns that existed between your mother and father while you were an infant and toddler. Like our native tongue, these patterns are imprinted deeply in our early programming long before we have a memory or choice.

Like language, any emotional expression or communication learned in childhood will remain the natural form of relating. It is a conditioned reflex. In times of stress or emotional intensity, an adult will usually regress not only to that early family-of-origin language, but also to that family's stress patterns. The way we handle stress is a conditioned reflex, too. In other words, as an adult, you will cuss or cry in English probably in the same manner one of your parents did, and probably for the same reasons.

Under stress, we all regress. It's just a question of to what, where, and whom we return. When our Inner Child surfaces under stress, what usually reappears is the early family-of-origin language with its programmed emotional interactional patterns and role model expectations of self and others. All Inner Child stress reactions will be based on the early childhood reality that was conditioned into each of us by our family-of-origin. The first imprint will remain as the first response simply because it is an automatic reflex.

What was familiar in childhood, we call our second nature when it is really our first nature. It's what comes naturally and automatically, without having to think about it first and decide what to say or do. It's familiar. So are your Inner Adult and Inner Mate patterns. **Remember, the greatest fear in adults is the fear of the unknown and the greatest comfort from fear is the known**. Under stress, you do what your Adult Role Model did.

Consistently, people will repeat these familiar behaviors rather than do something unfamiliar, even if the unfamiliar is a lot more comfortable. Often our parents' familiar feelings or behaviors are indeed highly uncomfortable, painful, unsatisfying, or problematic. Why would anyone want to keep on doing it then, you ask? Author Robert Anton Wilson says, "The imprint of the butterfly is already programmed into the caterpillar."

Likewise, the behavior of one of our parents is already programmed into each of us, ready and just waiting for the time when we will become one of the grownups. Think about it as data stored inside your own personal computer on a disk called your Inner Adult. The stress of puberty activates those subconscious Inner Adult files.

Puberty is the Inner Adult coming out of the Inner Child cocoon. Going from the familiar stage of childhood to adulthood is stressful simply because it is a such a big change and change is stressful simply because it brings on the unknown.

3. Will the Inner Adult Please Stand Up?

It is my belief, backed by more than a thousand case
studies, that your Inner Adult self is programmed by
your parents' relationship to know what to look for
years later in life when you search for an adult relationship of your own. **"Do what I say, not what I do,"
is an old parental proverb and, sure enough, we
do what they did, not what they said to do.** That's
the problem! Indeed, think of your parents' relationship
as a seed planted in childhood that doesn't bloom until
adulthood.

For a long time now we've have believed it is the
Inner Child part of the personality that picks a mate to
complete the child's unmet needs with one of the
parents. I think the Inner Adult picks the mate. What
has continually been overlooked by therapists is the
fact that the Inner Adult's experience of the other
parent's personality and behavior is often the same as
the Inner Child's. I've consistently found that people
who married someone like one parent were also very
much like the other in their relationship. That's why the
parent-child unmet need theory for mate selection is
right some of the time.

**That parent who was your Inner Adult Role
Model may also have had some of the same unmet
needs in his or her relationship with your Inner
Mate Model parent that you did as a child.** But the
needs that the Inner Adult model parent had with the
Inner Mate Model parent were adult-to-adult or parent-
to-parent relationship needs, not parent-child needs.
They're altogether different than your Inner Child's
unmet needs from that parent. We are referring to your
parents' unmet needs with each other. What is imbedded by example in your Inner Adult is your role model's
relationship patterns. What is imprinted is not only

that parent's unresolved conflicts, but the very same emotional scars, communication blocks, and unsuccessful interactional patterns that kept that parent from resolving the problems in his or her relationship.

Previous methods that have promised insights into choosing the right mate have failed simply because real conscious choice is not possible as long as we remain unaware of the programmed Inner Adult part of us that does the actual choosing. **Theories that say we marry someone who represents the parent with whom we have the most unmet needs come close, but miss the subtle but powerful truth: It's not how our mother or father was with us that determines whom we select for a mate. It's how our mother and father were in your early childhood with each other.**

That's why couples who are happy before they are married may begin to experience difficulty as they move to the husband-wife stage of their relationship, or later at the parenting stage. The trouble may start there simply because they had ineffective couple communication skills for that stage modeled during their childhood by their parents. It's very likely that the partners have different relationship models imbedded in their subconscious minds and these opposite programmed patterns are automatically surfacing now that they are married themselves. Negative or opposing interactional patterns won't work any better in this stage of their relationship than they did in the parents'. Most couples need positive precedents from their parents before they can even consider new solutions for themselves. The dilemma, of course, is how to get mutually cooperative parenting programming now.

The problem I've encountered in most relationships is that the Inner Adult in each partner subconsciously remembers how things should be in an adult relationship. Most couple responses are on automatic reflex.

That computer data was entered so long ago that you
may not even remember what it was until it comes out
of your own mouth and you hear yourself saying what
one parent said to the other.

For your Inner Adult, there is only one way to be
when you grow up and have a relationship. Be like
Mommy or Daddy. Find someone for the other role.
Have a relationship like theirs. Be like that Inner
Couple showed you (#8 on the Childhood History
Chart).

**This is what couples needed to work on in
therapy. Mom and Dad's interactional example.
Their relationship is what has been overlooked in
couple counseling up to now.** The Inner Couple was
the training film that you watched every day as a child.
Your parents had the two lead roles in this relationship
training film that gave you your first and only couple
imprint in your early years. As a result, you saw only
two models of how to be in a grown-up relationship.
Like him or like her. It's your very own home video of a
couple in action. When you grow up, you will play the
Inner Adult role. There are only two lead roles in this
film and in order for the replay to begin in your adulthood, you must first find someone to cast in the other
lead role, the Inner Mate.

**Invariably, people will pick the same type of
partner that their Inner Adult Role Model parent
picked, even if they consciously didn't know the
Inner Adult Role Model's reasons for that choice.**
They usually have the same reasons, needs, passions,
and feelings that their Inner Adult/parent did.

Remember: Your Inner Adult Role Model does not
have to be the parent of the same gender as you. It is
important to realize that we are talking not in gender-
bound terms, but in regard to adult personality and
behavior traits which, like height, do not show up until
adulthood. **When we get into our own adult rela-**

tionships, each of us will subconsciously interact as one of our parents did with his or her mate. Quite often, that Adult Role Model isn't the parent we thought it would be. But our conscious brain didn't decide this identification for us and may not even like being identified with that parent's personality and behaviors. Our Inner Adult programming contains our own personal set of instructions on how to be an adult and a programmed set of requirements for a certain type of mate to help us achieve our subconscious relationship model—the Inner Couple.

Both of Bill Clinton's Inner Adult role models were womanizers. His real father, William Jefferson Blythe, a traveling salesman, is reported to have left a girl in every town. Blythe had a shady past. Married four or five times, he had spent his life getting himself in and out of scrapes, using aliases, telling lies as he went. Driving recklessly on his way to visit his pregnant wife, he was killed several months before his son Bill was born. For the first three years of his life, young Bill lived with his maternal grandparents. Although they loved him dearly, Edith, quite an aggressive lady-about-town, and her alcoholic husband, were an abusive Inner Couple, and bad examples for Bill.

When he was four, Bill's mother, who had a reputation as a gambler, flirt, and flamboyant lady-about-town, married Roger Clinton, who was not only a gambler, but an alcoholic and a ladies' man with a history of wife abuse. Growing up with her parents had prepared Bill's mother for her abusive marriage to Roger. Now her son Bill was being imprinted with several Inner Adult and Mate models who would influence his future relationships negatively.

Jerome D. Levin, Ph.D., in his book "The Clinton Syndrome: The President and the Self-Destructive Nature of Sexual Addiction," describes a photograph in the Washington Post archives of Bill's mother in her twenties which bears a striking resemblance to Monica Lewinsky.

4. Who Do You Want to Be When You Grow Up?

In childhood, it was this Inner Adult part of your personality that identified with one of your parents. What that means is that as your personality began to develop, your emotional makeup and stress reactions turned out to be more like one of your parents than the other. So did your mating patterns.

Every other day we read in the newspaper where science has discovered a new gene. We can now accurately predict whether a person will develop a certain disease later in life or not. We say a person is predisposed by their genetic structure to be a certain way, not just up to the present moment, but throughout life. Height is a good example of a genetically programmed result that doesn't show up until adulthood. So are mating behavior and imprinted couple patterns.

Whether you believe in the theory of the Personality Gene or not, we see and hear about inherited physical traits every day in our normal family conversations. It is also common knowledge that particular personality traits run in families just like green eyes and curly hair do. A child can look like one parent and act like the other, or act like one parent and yet have a particular feature that reminds you of another family member. "My, my, he's got his momma's chin," or "You got that high I.Q. from your daddy, didn't you?" We say traits run in families. Certain health problems and the predisposition to alcoholism are only two of the inherited conditions that medical science recognizes as having been passed on from one generation to the next.

Psychogenetics is based on the belief that personality traits and emotional natures are inherited, like height or hair color, and that interactional pair bonds and patterns are the results of envi-

ronmental conditioning. It is not my intent to pursue here the long standing controversy, "Is it environment or heredity that determines a child's future?" I simply give you my opinion and offer you an option to believe, as Mark Twain and St. Augustine did, that it is the early environment that determines a child's later nature. "Give me a child until he is five and he is mine forever more," is how Twain states the impact that early conditioning has on the later adult.

So believe as you may, by nature or nurture, or both, the personality of one of your parents, relatives, or caretakers was most certainly imbedded in your developing psyche as a child, either before or after birth. In adulthood, you'll take after one of them in disposition, just like you'll take after one of them in hair color and height.

Role modeling from the adults in the early environment also has a lasting effect. Each child absorbs the idea that he or she is going to grow up like one of those early role models. "I'm going to be just like Mommy when I grow up," we hear a little girl say, and, lo and behold, years later, she isn't! Well, she looks exactly like Mother, she talks exactly like her, and she walks like her, but she's got her father's personality. Or we hear little boys say, "I want to marry someone like you, Mommy, when I grow up to be a Daddy." The example went in and you subconsciously, or consciously, modeled your adult relationship style after one of them. That parent is your Inner Adult.

About seventy-five percent of the time, when you grow up and your programming surfaces, the Inner Adult part of you chooses the same type of mate that your Adult Role Model parent chose— one like the other parent. If your personality is more like your father's, then he is your Inner Adult model and you will pick a mate like he did—someone with your mother's emotional makeup, because she is your Inner

Mate Model. If you are more like your mother, then she is your Inner Adult model and you will pick someone with your father's personality and behavior, no matter which gender you are. Then he would be your Inner Mate Model.

Psychogenetics and your mate selection process are not gender-bound, but personality-bound. We subconsciously copy the personality of one of our parents and then act it out in a relationship with someone like our other parent. We have chosen that person as a mate for her or his ability to interact in a very familiar pattern to our parents. The Selection Test you took in the beginning of this book bypasses your conscious mind and gets right to uncovering that Inner Adult part of you that contains all the early subconscious programming you absorbed about Mommy and Daddy in childhood. This is what makes the Selection Test such an amazing predictor of a budding relationship's future success. It reveals your Inner Mate programming too.

Remember that every day as a child you attended a training session on how to be in a relationship when you grew up. The training film was entitled, "What Mommies and Daddies Do." You had no choice but to watch it, adapt to it, and think all adult-adult relationships were like that. It wasn't until you went to school that you began to find out that other mommies and daddies weren't exactly like yours. As children, when we played grownups, we did what they did as mates and parents. We learned how to interact in each adult situation by watching them, and our play was practice for our adult roles later in life. You say that and I'll say this, just like Mommy and Daddy showed us.

Often it was harder to play mommies and daddies with friends in the neighborhood because they didn't know how to play right. Only your brothers and sisters did. They had watched the same training film you saw, and were already programmed to duplicate your parents' relationship interaction. It makes no difference that you may not have wanted to be like either of these parents or that you definitely did not want to marry someone like either of them. You did it anyhow!

As one female client said, "I married at seventeen to get away from my mother. As I look back on my four marriages, I've married my mother each time. They treated me the same way she did. It's as if she was here all along in spirit inside all my husbands. They were all like my awful mother. One and the same. I've spent ten years in therapy working on my Inner Child's relationship with my mother. Now you're telling me that all along, it's because I'm like my Dad that I've picked mates with my mother's personality. The real problem is that I'm attracted to the same kind of person my Dad was attracted to and so I naturally selected the same type of mate he did. Yikes!"

EXERCISE:

1. Look back at the Selection Test. The adult/parent that your current partner is most like is your Inner Mate Model and the other adult/parent is your Inner Adult Role Model, (either #2 or #3 on the Childhood History Chart). These identifications are not connected to gender, either yours or your parent's.

2. What personality and behavior traits of your Inner Adult parent do you recognize and already know you possess? Underline them on the test.

3. Was your Inner Adult Role Model your favorite parent?

4. What traits of your Inner Mate Model does your partner have? Underline them on the test.

5. Would you rather have had this parent as your Inner Adult Role Model?

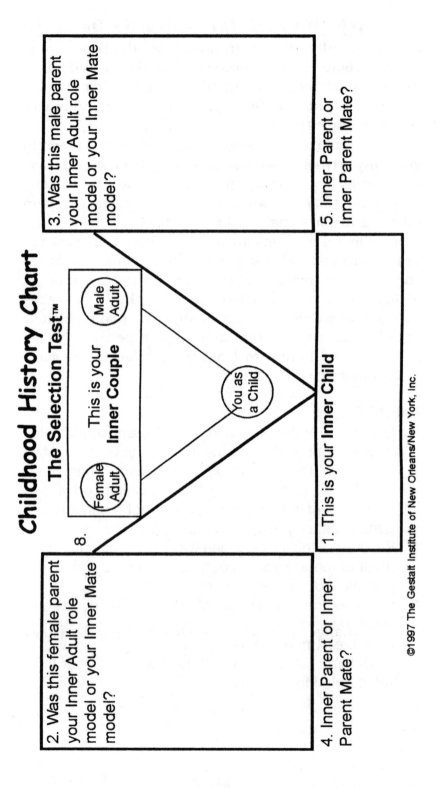

Childhood History Chart
The Selection Test™

2. Was this female parent your Inner Adult role model or your Inner Mate model?

3. Was this male parent your Inner Adult role model or your Inner Mate model?

8.

This is your **Inner Couple**

Female Adult

Male Adult

You as a Child

1. This is your **Inner Child**

4. Inner Parent or Inner Parent Mate?

5. Inner Parent or Inner Parent Mate?

5. *You and Your Role Models*

Let's explore the influences Adult Role Models and Mate Models have on our future coupling experiences. The term Inner Adult Role Model is the name given to the parent that you are most like in your current relationship and the Inner Mate Model is the parent that your partner is most like (either #2 or #3 on the Childhood History Chart).

If this Inner Adult/parent was also your favorite adult, you will prefer your role in this relationship because you will be more like the adult/parent you liked as a child and your self-esteem will be high.

If your favorite adult/parent was your Inner Mate Model, you will esteem your partner more than yourself in the relationship.

If you were fortunate enough to have had both parents (Inner Adult and Inner Mate Models) as favorites, you will feel good about both yourself and your partner in this relationship.

If you did not like either of your parents as the adults they were with each other, then your self-esteem and your esteem for your partner will be low. You will most likely prefer not being in a relationship and will feel better about yourself when you are single.

If your Inner Adult Role Model is marked plus on the Selection Test, then you have a positive example for yourself to follow as an adult. If minus, then you have a negative example, and you must reprogram your Inner Adult to change your Inner Couple relationship pattern.

Otherwise, in your couple relations, you (Inner Adult) will automatically imitate the attraction and interaction patterns of your Adult Role Model parent, and by doing so you will elicit your Mate Model parent's responses with your own mate (Inner Mate).

For instance, if your Inner Adult Role Model parent's

angry behavior with his or her mate was hated by you as a child, then your automatic repetition of that angry behavior with your Inner Mate will subconsciously retrigger the same hated reaction to yourself now that your Inner Child had to your Adult Role Model parent back in childhood.

But if your Adult Role Model was your favorite adult, as was Lisa's mother, and your Mate Model was hated by that favorite parent, you will also tend to hate your Inner Mate just as your Adult Role Model parent hated her mate.

The Inner Couple is the name given to the interactions that your Inner Adult Role Model and your Inner Mate Model had with each other in your childhood. It was the subconscious couple model for your adult-to-adult couple relationship when you grew up.

Once the mating process starts, your Inner Adult part is programmed to find someone like your Inner Mate Model parent. This Inner Mate Model is the type you are always attracted to, whether your conscious mind wants it to be that way or not. We are not talking about looks here. Someone new may look much like your Mate Model parent and not be anything like him or her. In order for that person to be your type, he or she must also have enough of the Inner Mate's personality and behavior traits.

The important factor here is whether this potential partner has the parental background necessary to interact with you the way your Inner Mate parent did with his or her mate; if not, even the most positive budding relationships will go no further. **The subconscious goal is to re-create the Inner Couple.**

Your mate was chosen by your Inner Adult programming to give you the same type of cues and response that your Adult Role Model parent received and to help you produce the same interactions your parents had with each other, good or bad.

6. As the Twig Is Bent, the Tree Shall Grow

As an example of what happens when people have positive Inner Couples, let's look at John and Mary Doe: Mary's Adult Role Model was her mother (#2), whom she described as a plus (+) on her Childhood History Chart and also as her favorite parent (#4).

As an adult woman, Mary described her mother as well liked by everyone in and outside of her family, and the kind of person and marriage partner Mary wanted to be. Her mother's parenting skills were excellent, too. Mary, therefore, had a gigantic head start in life. As an adult woman her self-image was high because she liked her mother, and her mother liked herself during Mary's impressionable childhood years. Her mother was both Mary's Inner Adult and Inner Parent role models (#2 and #4).

Predictably, Mary became the kind of positive adult, wife, and parent her mother was. She had an imprinted double whammy of positive self-talk, first in her Inner Child mind from her "plus" mother-child relationship (#6) and also from her mother's examples of high self-esteem as an adult person. Mary had high self-esteem now because her Adult Role Model mother (Inner Adult) did too when Mary was a young child. Mary also learned positive parenting skills from this adult as an Inner Parent role model (#4) and will therefore be able to rely on her instinctual responses in rearing her own children. (The #6 Mother-Child relationship was a plus).

Of course, Mary followed her mother's example and chose a mate like her own father, a kind loving man. John was picked because he matched Mary's Inner Mate/Father (#3). Like Mary's father, John was a "plus" adult person, a "plus" husband, and a "plus" parent (#5) to his young daughter. John was also a lucky child because he, too, received in his childhood what all chil-

dren are entitled to get from their parents but few actually do. John got his birthright—two emotionally
healthy, loving parents who had a positive couple relationship and positive individual and joint parenting
relationships with the child. Thus, in this best of all possible worlds, John's parents were able to hand down to
their son perfect Inner Couple and Inner Parenting programs, as he will to his children.

How did John fit into Mary's programming? John's
Inner Adult Role Model was also his mother (#2), but
the fact that both his and Mary's Inner Adults were
their mothers is not the reason he and Mary match.

John's same-gender parent, his father (#3), is his
Inner Mate Model and the kind of personality he recognized in Mary when he first met her. "I just knew Mary
would make a great wife and mother for my children,"
John said without consciously realizing his Inner
Mate/Father was his personality model when he picked
Mary. Like his mother, John was searching for a marriage partner with the positive, loving traits his father
had. John himself was programmed to exhibit his
mother's "plus" interactional traits with Mary, a mate
like his father.

If instead both Mary and John's Adult Role Models
had been marked minus as adults, mates, or parents,
there would be corresponding negative effects in the
lives of this couple. If either Mary or John had a "minus"
parental set, it is unlikely that they would ever have
been attracted to each other in the first place. If they
had, it would be highly improbable that their relationship would ever have progressed far enough past the
dating stage for them to even get married, simply
because their parental sets were not a match. Couple
trouble was not programmed into either Mary or John's
Inner Couple expectations. Only a partner programmed
for a happy marriage would be marked suitable on each
one's subconscious score sheet.

Note: Due to the placement of #2 mother/female parent on the left hand side of the chart and #3 father/male parent on the right, if either Mary or John had identified his or her father as the Inner Adult, then, of course, the #2 section of the chart would be for the Inner Mate and the #3 section would be for the Inner Adult.

7. *Will the Inner Couple Please Do Something Different?*

Like Mary and John, the relationship you observed in your early home environment from birth to five years of age was the primary image of an adult-adult relationship on the impressionable screen of your subconscious mind.

Remember that none of us ever experienced our parents before they were Mother and Father. By the time you arrived, your parents had certainly already had sex at least once. They were in, or had been in, a physically intimate relationship. That relationship between these two primary people in your life is imprinted just as strongly in your subconscious mind as is your native tongue. That's why I call this interactional program the Inner Couple.

Your mother and father's relationship, like it or not, became the basis for all later intimate relationships between you and other human beings in your adult life. Since there were only these two lead roles in their relationship example, you will take after one of these adults more than the other. Psychogenetics says that your Adult Role Model parent is more than just your second nature in adulthood. Inside the Inner Couple, it becomes your first nature.

Just like your native tongue, this set of imprinted adult personality traits and its set of cues and responses to its Inner Mate are implanted in childhood long before you have an opportunity to decide if you want them there. Plus or minus, this parent's patterns form the basis for what you will experience later in your own intimate relationships with your mates or mate.

Your subconscious not only tell you how to interact with a partner, but also what type of partner to select.

It may cause you grief to know your partner was a programmed selection. The set of instructions that led you to pick the mate you did was in every sense of the phrase a *post-hypnotic suggestion* because it functioned without your conscious awareness, controlling whom you would attract, select, and marry. If you don't believe me, try to think in another language besides English. You literally have no choice as long as you remain unaware of your programming. You only have one option. Speak like them. Be like them.

If you happened to be raised in a bilingual home, you have two choices of languages in which to think as an adult. If you had two sets of parents or caretakers in your early childhood, you have alternate role models. Nevertheless, all memories of your childhood and your parents' interaction are recorded in your native language. It is those parents in your childhood who formed the basis for your Inner Couple.

EXERCISE:

1. Turn back to the Selection Test in the beginning of the book. Look at the description of your mother and father's relationship when you were a child. Is your relationship with your current partner similar to their Inner Couple model (#8 on Childhood History Chart)?
2. Was your relationship with past partner similar? What about any former partners?
3. What personality traits are similar about you and your Inner Adult Role Model parent?
4. About your current partner and your Inner Mate Model parent? And your former partners?

THE MOMMY AND DADDY TRAINING FILM

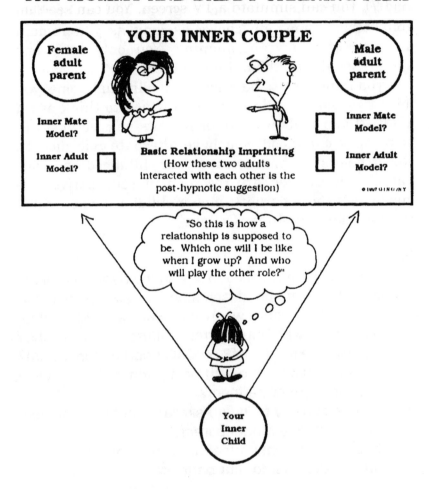

8. Watching Home Movies

Let's look at that Selection Test another way. If you draw a big square around the interaction between your parents, (#8 on the Childhood History Chart on pages 6 and 7), you can simulate a TV screen. You can see that as a child you were the viewing audience watching your parents' interactions on that screen. What you saw daily was a relationship training film, a home movie starring your parents in the lead roles. Your relationship now is simply a replay of that old script handed down from generation to generation.

It was becoming increasingly obvious to me that none of us have any inside experience of our Adult Role Models in relationship to their mates. In order to uncover the Inner Couple pattern, it would be necessary to walk a mile in their moccasins, rather than just remember how those people had acted with each other back then.

Years ago, Eric Berne first introduced the concept of relationship scripts in his classic book *Games People Play* and Transactional Analysis was born. Claude Steiner followed with *Scripts People Live*. Both explained the subconscious patterns in relationships that produce negative outcomes.

By the end of this book, you will have the opportunity to rewrite any negative couple scripts you have acquired. You can learn to interact in more effective ways than your parents did and create the relationship you always dreamed of having with your partner. Later in the book, I will give you some exercises to change your Inner Couple programming.

First, however, you'll have to learn to consciously impersonate your parents as the adults they were, instead of subconsciously impersonating them in your own relationships. It is necessary that you roleplay your parents once as they were and once as you wanted them to be in their relationship. Roleplaying is the most important step in the Psychogenetic process of reprogramming the Inner Couple on the screen in your subconscious memory. Roleplay allows you a high degree of intuitive access into your subconscious Inner Couple files, access you cannot get through conscious memory.

9. Voices from the Past

Years ago on the Johnny Carson television show, I watched in fascination as Rich Little went into the specifics of how he created an impersonation. First, the popular impersonator watched his subjects move and talk until he isolated particular gestures and postures most frequently used in their behavior. For example, Rich identified several physical expressions that were repetitive in Jack Benny's routine. Demonstrating, the impersonator stood up, crossed his arms in front of his chest, tilted his head to one side, looked up with his eyes, and smirked with one side of his mouth.

There was something vaguely familiar about that posture, I thought as I smiled, even though I couldn't remember what it meant at first. I liked the feeling of seeing it again, even though Jack Benny wasn't doing it. As you are reading this, you may already be getting a picture from memory of Jack Benny's expression. Perhaps you are remembering that Benny used to say "Well!" when he assumed that posture. Most people are totally unaware of tonality and their subconscious memory of voices, especially ones they heard in their childhood.

Jack's repertoire also included references to his age—thirty-nine, of course—and his relationships with his wife and a black man named . . . is your memory improving? If you are one of the millions who grew up watching Jack Benny, I guarantee that if you stand up and roleplay Jack doing all of those postures, you can access your feeling memory of Mary Livingston and Rochester ten times more readily than you ever thought possible.

"Johnny Carson has his golf swing and his pencil tap. He straightens his tie. He leans back in his chair," Rich Little continued. The TV public's associations with those behaviors of Johnny's are so strong that if an impersonator does any two of these things together, most late night TV viewers will automatically begin to feel the way they felt back when they actually watched Johnny on TV. In effect, they are watching him on the TV screen of their mind as they look at the impersonator.

Johnny's audience not only remembers who he is but also knows what to expect the minute they hear "He-e-e-re's ... Johnny!" In their subconscious minds, they are already anticipating the Carson monologue. Those expectations were created by pattern repetition.

Imbedded, imprinted, or inherited, interactional patterns in one's family of origin are exactly like that. Becoming an adult is like saying, "He-e-e-re's Mommy!" or "He-e-e-re's Daddy!" It's our parents we are subconsciously impersonating now. You are programmed to repeat your parents' relationship whether you like it or not. That is, unless you remake the old film or change the channel to a more positive Inner Couple pattern.

QUESTIONS:
1. Was your parents' early couple relationship a comedy, a drama, an adventure film, a religious story, or a tragedy?
2. Was it filled with fun, passion, love, rage, fear, terror, pain, grief, laughter, joy, or disappointment?
3. Is your Inner Couple supposed to laugh, fight, drink, love, leave, or cry?
4. Which partner has the power, the brains, the looks, the money?
5. Do you like the beginning, the middle, or the ending?
6. What is the title of your parents' home video? And yours?

IV. THE PATTERN

Just remembering that our parents could not teach us advanced relationship skills is enough to soften your heart and forgive yourself and your partner for the mistakes you repeatedly make.

—*John Gray*

1. It Runs in the Family

We expect that members of the same family will look alike. Most often the child will have the same eye and hair color, height, and facial features as one of the parents. But what about disposition? Or talents? They usually show up too, but for years we have assumed it was early environment and not heredity that accounted for those traits. More recently, research in genetics has suggested the existence of personality genes.

Psychogenetics says one parent's disposition will predominate in each child; the other's personality will also be imprinted, but it will be recessive or secondary. People ask me, "Do you really think I've inherited one of my parent's personalities? Aren't I a mixture of the qualities of both?" Yes, of course, physically that is often true, but you are a combination of specific traits and not a mixture.

Let's compare Psychogenetics to genetics. Studies on identical twins separated at birth reveal that in adult life such twins display an amazing similarity to each other and their parents, not only in appearance, but also in personality, lifestyle, talent, emotions, and behavior—even though they were raised in different environments. Despite their different paths, their adult

83

lives lend credence to the suspicion that some things may be pre-set or predetermined in the fetal stage, or that there is some early imprinting inside the human being that sets people from the same family on amazingly similar courses in adulthood.

Most of us are ready to agree that children inherit certain predispositions. Doctors take family histories to predict which of these familiar physical strengths and weaknesses may show up in adulthood. Insurance companies bet on the accuracy of these inherited tendencies and therefore are sticklers for all the health information they can get about the parents. Medically, it is possible to predict the future from the past, at least statistically. Psychogenetically it is, too.

Parents recognize that newborn babies exhibit distinct personality traits. "She's just like her father. Just wants to eat and sleep. Her brother was like me, into everything." Some babies are restless, others content. Some are easy to take care of, others finicky. As the child develops, more and more of the uniqueness of that individual is apparent. "It's in her nature," we say, or "You can tell she's her father's child with that temper."

I've always liked the word *apparent*. In this context, it is most appropriate. "A-parent" is what I think every time I see or hear it. What shows up is what the lineage put into the composition of that human being. Most of the time, like begets like—at least like one of the parents or one of the relatives. Some traits like eye color are immediately obvious in childhood, while others, like height, temperament, talents, and preferences, don't manifest until adulthood.

Every day we open the paper to read that another gene has been discovered. Psychogenetics is based on the belief that personality traits are inherited. I believe that a full spectrum of personality genes will soon be discovered and through DNA testing this will allow us to immediately identify the inborn nature of the young child and predict the personality of the future adult.

Adult behavior seems to be influenced by repeated examples from the role models in our childhood, which were hypnotized into our subconscious early on. Genetics predisposes us toward certain traits. Environment influences behavior. The combination produces chips off the old block and apples that don't fall far from the tree. One of the familiar brain teasers is the old question, "Is the glass half full or half empty?" Well, of course, it's both. We are strongly influenced both by our inherited dispositions and our early environmental examples.

Couple scripts are also repeated generation after generation. From birth to five years of age, you got a total subconscious imprinting. From five to ten, you may have some conscious memory of your parents' relationship, but it does not have the full behavioral imprint that the first five years have on your Inner Couple.

Many people have asked me if the relationship between their parents during their teenage years had any impact at all. The parental imprints from adolescence on have a lesser impact because we remember them consciously. But even though as a teenager you may have rebelled against your parents, the Inner Couple imprint from the early years will surface. In your adult-adult relationships, you will become like one of them and tend to relate to your mate the same way that person did to his or her mate.

2. *Betwixt and Between, It's What's on the Screen*

What appears to be true is that attraction and mating bonds echo the example set by the primary parental pair in our early family-of-origin. As children, we absorbed not just the interactional imprint of our Inner Adult Role Model and the Inner Mate Model, but their initial attraction to each other, and the emotional energy *between* the two. Somehow their mating dance was also programmed into our subconscious mind, even though we weren't around to see it. As adults we usually repeated their storylines and found someone like our other parent (the Inner Mate Model). The stage is then set for us to automatically interact with our own mates in the same patterns that our role model parents interacted with theirs.

What is even more amazing, is that our mate's parents' early relationship usually matches our own parents' patterns. The in-law pair bonds are usually composed of similar sets, one parent like this and one parent like that, just like yours. If your parents were a set of opposites, your in-laws are likely to be too. If your couple sets are alike, your in-laws will be, too. Consistently, people will pick partners who have parents with the same interactional husband-wife patterns, and who have the same relationship imperative to recreate the same Inner Couple pattern. Whether both parents are alike or both parents are opposites, they will usually contain similar personality sets. One like this and one like that.

Mary Jo and Don were the first couple to ever work on their parents' relationship with me. Psychogenetics was a new way to look at this troubled couple's pair bond. I set up two empty chairs and asked them one at a time to interact as their parents had in order to give me a demonstration of each one's Inner Couple programming. And interact they did. Alternately, they took turns roleplaying their parents, and by doing so they uncovered forgotten childhood memories of their parents. Wanting them to do more then just see their parents' behavior as they had in childhood, I asked them, one at a time, to occupy the third empty chair.

"Be your Inner Child/self and tell your parents how you felt as a child—when you watched their training film on how to be a couple," I suggested.

Both Mary Jo and Don realized how much they disliked what they had seen as kids. They wished they could change what their parents were doing up on that screen in their memory. Changing them in memory was such a good idea, we decided to do just that. I asked them to reenact their parents' relationship as they wanted it to be. It was their chance to stop wishing their parents' relationships had been different and remake those home movies themselves.

Years ago in an Erhard Seminar Training (EST) session, I heard a phrase that kept coming back to mind. Werner Erhard, the founder of EST, used to say that "In order for change to occur, we have to first create a space inside for something different to happen." Years later, Richard Bandler, co-developer of Neurolinguistic Programming, invented a reprogramming technique he called the Change History Pattern. Both these concepts opened my mind to creating new possibilities in a client's history. I liked the idea of fulfilling the Inner Child's wish to have the parental couple be happy with each other.

In the Wish Fulfillment Exercise I used with Mary Jo and Don, we actually created alternate memories through roleplaying their parents differently. I could feel the excitement of a new solution emerging in my work. I had been trained in Gestalt to use two-chair dialogues, having the Inner Child talk to a parent to resolve the adult client's parent-child unfinished business. Instead, Mary Jo and Don were resolving *their* husband-wife unfinished business in the same way as their Inner Child selves wanted their parents to do for themselves.

From then on, I began suggesting to my other clients that they also roleplay their parents fixing their relationship with each other, in order to create a precedent inside their own memories. Practicing this new experience of their parents resolving their relationship would make it easier for my clients to be different with each other now.

The technique worked so well I stopped dealing with my other clients' current relationships and focused instead on their parental imprints. The more my clients did the repair work on their parents' relationships, the faster their current relationships with each other automatically changed.

Sitting in the third chair had given Mary Jo and Don the awesome opportunity to watch their parents create and demonstrate a happy solution. Several times, each of them told their parents just how wonderful they felt seeing them happy with each other, finally. Still speaking as their parents, *they* thanked Mary Jo and Don for giving them a better solution for their own marriage, without realizing that *they*, Mary Jo and Don, had given themselves this solution. By being willing to imagine how their parents would have been if they had possessed better relationship skills, Mary Jo and Don were able to utilize these skills for themselves and hand them down to their daughter.

"I never, ever dreamed things could change that much and be that good for us together," Don said. "And so easily, too. It's a dream come true."

QUESTIONS:
1. Imagine you are a child again. How would you like each of your parents to be with each other?
2. Who would have to be different first?

3. Matching Inner Couples

Herb and Leslie came in to see me just as I was formulating my Psychogenetic theory. Now I finally understood the pairings that had happened in those Relationship Workshops years before. Imprinted Inner Couple patterns had controlled how those participants behaved and felt in their current relationships. Subconscious programs had activated and limited their interactions and still remained in place, no matter what they had learned consciously in the workshops.

It was becoming clear to me that in order for couples to change permanently, they had to learn the new behaviors on a subconscious level as Mary Jo and Don had done. That meant having them *re*-solve their parents' unsatisfactory relationships themselves instead of just wishing their parents had.

So as Herb and Leslie told me about their differences, I began listening for similarities in their parents' relationships. I looked for ways in which their Inner Couple issues and interactions were the same. The conflict in Herb and Leslie's current relationship surely reflected the unresolved issues in both of their parents' couple relationships. Unless we fixed the original conflicts from those past relationships, we would simply be whitewashing the broken fence in Herb and Leslie's. But with no positive behavioral precedent from their Inner Couple role models, neither Herb nor Leslie would be able to maintain the conscious change they wanted to achieve, no matter how hard they tried.

At the first sign of stress, Herb or Leslie, or both, would regress to their programmed Inner Couple behavior. One partner would automatically retrigger the other, since both their Mate Models had similar reactive programming. Together, Herb and Leslie contained all the imprinting they needed to replicate their parents' troubled relationship—and were doing just that.

Herb and Leslie's selection of each other was most certainly not a conscious decision. As they both admitted, neither had married the partner they liked the best or loved the most. Even though they knew they were not good to or for each other, their parents' past had compelled them to choose a person who matched their Inner Mate Models. No one, no matter how much nicer, more attractive, smarter, richer, or more attentive, could have been accepted by either Herb or Leslie's Inner Adults. Like many couples who break up for reasons they cannot understand, Herb and Leslie had not been able to understand why they had both ended relationships with more loving partners to be with each other. The Selection Test showed them how they had followed their unhappy Inner Couples' conditioning. Like a set of mirrors, their Inner Adult and Inner Mate Models were a matched set of unhappiness from previous generations.

Even if the Inner Child in each of them was trying to fix their parents' problems, their Inner Adults picked the same kinds of mates, that were guaranteed to keep them troubled. And to make matters worse, they were using the same ineffective problem-solving methods that hadn't worked for their parents. The couple had been drawn to each other because their Inner Couple scripts were so similar. Certainly not perfect mates for each other, they were however a perfect match.

Indeed, I had many other clients who wondered why they had broken up with someone they loved, who also loved them, to choose instead a neglectful partner. The Psychogenetic answer was simple. Their Inner Mate parent was unloving to their Inner Adult parent, so being with a loving mate did not fit their Inner Couple mold. **The concept of the imprinted Inner Couple is the answer to why some people stay friends but** do not become lovers, why some lovers never get along once they are married, why people who argue all the time stay together, and why people who love each other marry someone else. It's the answer to why opposites attract. Their parents were opposites, too.

4. What "Opposites" Really Means

It has been my experience as a couple counselor for over two decades that, with few exceptions, couples who get into trouble consistently are opposites and had parents and grandparents who were opposites, too. Originally the phrase *opposites attract* meant *opposite genders,* but we no longer think about it that way. Today, when people say *opposites attract,* what they usually are referring to is two people with distinctly different personality types. One introvert and one extrovert, one nice and one mean, one drunk and one sober, etc. When a relationship doesn't work, you'll hear people say, "I'm picking someone exactly opposite next time." But the subconscious mind has a different meaning for the word *opposite.*

In a child's mind, the other parent is the opposite. Our parents stood side by side, or as we say, opposite each other. What happens when we consciously decide to pick someone opposite from our previous partner, is that we switch over to that other parent role model in our new relationship. We often adopt the other parent's role in the couple relationship to avoid picking the same type of partner again. Remember, there usually aren't any other Adult Role Models from which to choose, except the other parent.

However, taking on the Inner Mate's role the next time, with all the personality and behavioral characteristics of the other parent in the Inner Couple (the secondary personality), simply causes you to pick a new partner like the Inner Adult/parent you just were in your previous relationship. Unfortunately, even though the decision to switch role models is made in order to avoid the same negative relationship outcome, the combination of one like Mom and one like Dad once again produces the same Inner Couple outcome. When you choose the opposite role, you only become more like the opposite parent yourself and react with the same pro- grammed behaviors as this other parent would. Switching roles is not the solution. Often it is like jumping out of the frying pan into the fire.

EXERCISE:
1. List the behavior and the personality traits of your parents and both sets of grandparents.
2. Would you describe these couples as opposites? Or "alikes"?
3. Have your mate list the traits of his or her parents and grandparents, too.

5. *Switching Role Models*

Gloria was a typical example of role switching. Her favorite parent was her mother, who was devoted, friendly, and yet very demanding. Gloria had very little satisfying communication with her father, her Inner Mate Model parent. He was cold, sullen all the time, busy, distant, and physically abusive when he drank. Gloria's parents argued all the time, were cold to each other, and never did anything together but fight.

"My mother would cry and my father would leave for days. That was their idea of resolving a problem."

Current parent-child theories of mate selection would say that Gloria's Inner Child would chose as her marriage partner someone with whom she has the same unmet needs she had with her father. But Gloria married her childhood sweetheart of ten years, someone she knew well, who had always been loving to her. No matter how close they were all those years before they married, sure enough, he and Gloria started arguing soon after they were married and never got along anymore.

"Dean got even colder to me and started drinking with his buddies the minute I got pregnant. Why? He wasn't like that before," Gloria told me. "I just couldn't take it anymore."

The second time Gloria married, she said, "I made sure I picked someone very different from my father. In fact, just to be doubly sure, I picked someone the exact opposite of Dean." But her marriage to Al turned out the same anyway—arguments, insults, coldness, separateness.

Now the big question: How did Gloria get the same couple outcome the second go-round? We know the answer already. Gloria switched from her Inner Adult to her Inner Mate Model. She picked someone like her devoted mother for a mate the second time around. Much to her surprise, in the second marriage, it was Gloria who became cold, angry, withdrawn, and abusive, not Al.

"I even started to drink. I became everything I disliked in my father," she said.

Of course her father was now her Inner Adult, and he drank! In other words, the parent with whom she'd had the most unmet needs, much to her surprise, showed up in her, not in her partner. In her father's role now, Gloria didn't like either her Inner Adult/self or her devoted Inner Mate/partner.

Interesting, considering the parent whom Gloria liked the most as a child was her devoted mother. But her mother's perfect devotion only aggravated Gloria, who was now playing her father's role. In her first marriage, Gloria's mother had been her Inner Adult Role Model. Now her mother was her Inner Mate Model and Goria was reacting as her father had.

Finally I was able to explain why succeeding relationships often turned out like the first one, only reversed. The person had switched roles. When the parents were opposites on the Selection Test, people unwittingly got back into the same kind of abusive relationship in their second marriage by marrying someone completely opposite their first partner.

As a result of our counseling sessions, Gloria understood why she had pushed Al away. In this marriage, Gloria's mother's role was played by her second husband and Gloria was left having to be like her father.

"As a child, when I saw the pain my father's coldness caused my mother, little could I have imagined I'd be treating my husband that way. I don't even like myself when I drink. He's been so good to me, but he's so goody-goody. Now that I know what's making me act like this, how can I stop it?" Gloria pleaded.

I couldn't tell her. All I knew was it hadn't made any sense for them to get together in the first place. Opposites rarely produce happy couples.

6. Falling in Love

I had to wonder why opposites were so attracted to each other. Why were they so quick to fall "in love" when they weren't even "in like"? Even at a young age, the fascination with difference was confusing to me. In grammar school, I had girl friends that I liked mainly because they were like me. We usually agreed on everything, and when we reached the teenage years, it became mandatory. We dressed alike, talked alike, did things together, liked the same rock stars, but we didn't always agree on boys.

Somewhere along the line, we had gotten different messages about boys and no one could predict who would like whom. "He's a creep, Patsy," I'd say. "What do you ever see in him?" How she could like Buck, I'll never know. His personality wasn't anything like hers or mine. But Patsy did like him, and she wondered what I saw in the boy who fascinated me. "Fascinated" is a good tip off here.

Teenage crushes are intense obsessions that alternately produce longing and anxiety. Overreactions are the order of the day, and we chalk it all up to hormones. We chalk a lot up to hormones, in fact, and later in life, we explain away the mating game as "chemistry." The word *chemistry* identifies the set of unique, unexplainable internal and external overreactions we have to a particular person at a given time in our lives. It is possible to have the same "chemistry" at another time with another person, but impossible to have two intense obsessions simultaneously with two different people. It smacks of disloyalty to even suggest such a thing. Dedication, devotion, and desire are all part of the same package directed to the crush object.

The term *infatuation* is often used to keep feelings from being confused with love—real love. Real love is synonymous with marriage or being in love. Of course, the term *in love* is used regularly to describe infatuation, which is the result of "chemistry." I've come to think of it all as hypnosis. The person in love is under a spell. *In love* is *in a trance*, and these intense feelings, of course, are stressful.

EXERCISE:

Here are some common words and phrases that we use to describe the experience of falling in love. Fill in the blanks to see which trances apply to you.

I was entranced by _____.

I'm intrigued by _____.

I'm under the spell of _____.

I'm fascinated by _____.

There was something about the way _____.

For some reason I can't explain, I _____.

I fell for _____.

I was drawn to _____.

I can't think of anything else but _____.

I was charmed by _____.

I succumbed to _____.

I just got lost in _____.

I fell hopelessly in love with _____.

I'm captivated by _____.

I was enthralled by _____.

I'm in a daze over _____.

I can't get away from _____.

He's the _____ of my dreams.

I can't take my eyes off of _____.

I knew the minute I saw _____.

I love the way _____ makes me feel.

7. Post-Hypnotic Suggestion

Most of us know what it feels like to be in love. There's that far away look, the constant concentration on your beloved, the knowledge that everything you ever wanted has rolled itself up into this perfect person. There's that feeling that no one on earth has ever felt this way before and the mad certainty that this feeling you have will last forever. Love is ecstasy and agony, freedom and slavery and entrapment, a fulfillment of our most secret dreams. In fact, we fall in love much the way we fall asleep. We go from one internal state of being to another. "In love" is a dream state, a subconscious feeling.

Sigmund Freud actually compared the experience of being hypnotized to the feeling of being in love. He also related the behavior of the hypnotized subject toward the hypnotist as much like the behavior members of a primal group have toward their leader, because the subject follows the suggestion of the hypnotist automatically, without making a conscious decision to do so. People in love do that, too. Are they hypnotized, and by whom?

Some old dictionaries define hypnosis as a trance-like state characterized by an exaggerated suggestibility and a temporary interruption of the normal functions of memory, personality, and perception. The hypnotic state also can be self-induced by concentration on a single thought, object, or person, in which case the phenomenon is called auto-hypnosis or auto-suggestion. Plain and simple, this means a person can go into trance simply by focusing on one person, remembering certain stimuli, or repeating previous trance behaviors. Stress or sudden change can also produce regressed behaviors, as can intense feelings.

Hypnosis is also used to induce age regression to the

time of a previous event, and can bring up repressed feelings that lie hidden in the subconscious. During hypnosis, the conscious mind steps out of the way and the subconscious takes over. We call this a trance. The possibilities of hypnosis are without limitations.

Our modern-day ad campaigns are a good example of post-hypnotic suggestion by repetition. The more we see a certain product advertised, the more we want to buy it. "You can't eat just one," said the potato chip commercial. We become conditioned to believe a certain product will produce a certain effect.

Pavlov's studies on classical conditioning explored the associations made in the dog's mind to the sound of a bell. Simply because a bell had been rung each time the dog was fed, now the sound of the bell alone was enough to trigger the dog's salivation response. This is called stimulus-response, regression, and trance.

Pavlov's dog's reaction was association by repetition. We learn by repetition, too. Often our reactions to stimuli are compulsive, and outside our conscious mind's control. Most often these reactions are from our family-of-origin imprinting.

Post-hypnotic suggestion produces a stimulus-response pattern in the brain. A prior suggestion or command to our subconscious can take over and produce a response in us, without our knowing from what, whom, or where the original stimulus came. **Most of the time the hypnotists were our parents in our early childhood. They induced the first trance.** We just respond the way we were programmed without ever being able to remember why we behave that way. Recently, researchers have begun to study love's evolutionary origins to find out whether it is encoded in the genes or imprinted in the brain. Are we in love with what we first saw? Was it love at first sight . . . or at first sound? At first touch, or taste, or smell? Or all of the above?

8. Inner Childhood

Psychotherapists have developed techniques called Inner Child dialogues that help the average adult recover some of the early family-of-origin subconscious imprinting. More and more we are finding that the memories from childhood that are the most damaging are the ones that the conscious mind couldn't resolve or talk about to anyone at the time. Often the child had to keep bad feelings secret.

Our early memory contains both good and bad feelings. Events that happened to us and around us are imprinted in the subconscious mind. The more unpleasant the memories, the more the tendency to forget the whole thing. Forgetting simply means not being able to recall it. The feelings associated with the event were buried inside, and unfortunately, they were buried alive. It is these buried feelings that seem to jump up out of nowhere and interfere with our current lives, our decisions and our adult relationships. They get us in trouble without our understanding why.

"I don't know why I said that," we hear ourselves wondering out loud. "It was stupid of me." Have you ever promised yourself you wouldn't repeat a certain behavior, and then found yourself doing exactly what you swore you wouldn't do? "She was only trying to be nice to me. But I jumped down her throat. I'm driving people I love away from me. It makes no sense," is a common example of such a dilemma.

Most things buried in the subconscious mind make no sense to the conscious mind. In fact, it dumped those feelings there because they made no sense in the first place. The conscious mind doesn't even remember burying them. They have been buried since childhood, because the child you were then was unable to deal with those feelings and repressed them.

One of the biggest categories of things that make no sense to the childhood conscious mind is adult-to-adult relationships. Not yet having been an adult, you had neither the life experiences nor the comprehension to understand what was going on between the parents you loved and depended on so much. Yet these are the very people you emulate when you become an adult, and you do so without ever really understanding why. "Before the Selection Test, all I got from therapy was how my partner and I should behave as a married couple. We never knew why we did what we did to each other. Now all we have to do is look at the training film that each of us watched daily from birth to five years old, to see how we are under stress."

What Inner Child dialogues often uncover is our earliest imprint of what an adult-to-adult relationship is supposed to be like—a model that became our subconscious goal for adulthood. How do you play Mommy or Daddy? One like this, one like that. Each of us subconsciously knows what a couple relationship is like. It's what our parent-to-parent relationship was like; you still know even if you no longer remember how they interacted—in fact, especially if you don't remember.

The feelings between you and your mate and the feelings between your parents must match. Remember, that Inner Couple seed was planted by repetitious example. The very act of getting married heightens the Psychogenetic trance hiding in the Inner Adult part of you. Already in place, the Inner Couple program is activated when the mating process begins. **Your relationship will go only as far as this old programming can take it, and no further—unless you can get out of your trance and purposefully override that post-hypnotic suggestion.**

QUESTIONS:

1. What don't you understand about yourself in adult relationships?
2. What didn't you understand about your partner or former partners?
3. What didn't you understand about your own parents' relationships?

9. Under Stress, We All Regress

In the beginning of this book, I gave you an assignment designed to put you in stress. I only gave you ten minutes to complete Step One of the Selection Test, something most people could not do. I did this to discourage you from thinking too much about your answers, so that we could access your subconscious childhood memories more easily.

Under any kind of stress, most people automatically regress to their programmed patterns. Regression is a form of trance. Stress of any kind induces regression back to the coping behaviors learned in childhood, the ones the adults in your family-of-origin practiced daily, and which you learned from your Inner Adult Role Model. These are the same behaviors you now automatically exhibit during any kind of test or stress.

Whatever was going on in your Adult Role Model's life during your first five years was imprinted in your subconscious memory (Inner Adult). That's why siblings will often show a different experience of your same parents on their Selection Test. Each sibling's early childhood experience (especially before two years of age), reflects a different period in their Adult Role Model's life and their parents' relationship. What shows up on each person's Inner Couple screen is how their parents were during that person's first five years.

Although Mom and Dad's methods and interactions may not have been ideal for a happy couple with a normal family life, it was all you knew. Even though Mom and Dad's ways may have been different from your neighbors', as a toddler you didn't know anybody else's ways. The way your parents acted with you and each other was imprinted in your mind's eye. In fact, everyone in your early family-of-origin had a significant impact on you, whether you liked their behavior or not.

The interactions from the world you grew up in were so deeply imbedded into your subconscious mind by the time you were five years old, we could easily say you were hypnotized by them.

And what difference does all that make now? It's all over and done with, or is it? Most of us no longer consciously remember much from our first five years of life, if anything at all, and you may have had a difficult time recalling how you felt as a young child or even where you lived then. Those events, places, and feelings were stored deep in your subconscious memory under B for Best Left Forgotten. But under stress you do what your Inner Adult Role Model did.

It is therefore important that you become aware of your childhood, especially what was going on at home before you went to kindergarten or first grade. The Selection Test lets you recognize what stress reactions were imprinted inside your subconscious mind. As the "Recovery Community" says, "What do you do when you get Hungry, Angry, Lonely, or Tired? H.A.L.T.!" People recovering from addiction often respond to stress by returning to their avoidance behavior; they go back to drinking or taking drugs. That's how they handle stress, by regressing.

Bill Clinton is an example of a person who rose above his childhood role models in his professional life but regressed to both his Inner Adults' behaviors under stress. Already mourning the deaths of three significant adults in his life, his mother, a father figure, and a close friend, and given that Clinton knew he was already under investigation in the Paula Jones case, the fact that Clinton got involved with Monica Lewinsky at all, was risky...but in the White House? However, sex addiction and gambling are both high-risk and sensation-seeking behaviors. Blythe, Bill's father, was killed at fifty-two due to his reckless driving, passing cars at high speed, he spun off the road in a rush to see his pregnant wife, and Roger Clinton was a gambler.

QUESTIONS:

1. How did you deal with the stress of completing the ten-minute Selection Test? The exercises?

2. Did you give up, try to finish in time, go over the time limit and feel guilty about it, get mad, or feel compelled to do it right?

3. Have you gotten interested, aggravated, exhausted, or challenged at each exercise? Did you skip over them?

4. Which parent would react this way under stress?

10. How to Find Your Type

The fact that imprinted personalities are not gender-bound, and stress reactions are especially parent-bound, was becoming more and more obvious to me. **Adult-adult interactions are not determined by one's parent-child relationships in childhood, but by the example of the parents' relationship with each other.** These insights have formed the foundation of the Psychogenetic System of couple counseling.

Adult love relationships are very parent-bound. Indeed, one of our parents is still picking our mates. Somehow we need to gain more choice before we fell in love.

As Carl Jung said, "That which is hidden deep inside of us will manifest itself as fate." I realized that there was only one way to find out what was hidden deep inside . . . we had to first find out what had already manifested itself as fate in our **other** relationships.

EXERCISE:

1. On the Relationship Wheel on the next page, put your name inside the center circle and then list each of the relationship partners you have had in chronological order inside the surrounding circles. Identify them as plus (+) or minus (–).
2. Write several personality and behavioral traits of each partner in his or her circle. Also note physical characteristics.
3. Identify each partner as being more like your mother or more like your father by placing M or F in each circle.
4. Put the other parent's initial inside the center of your Self circle.
5. Which parent is the Inner Adult hiding inside you in each relationship?

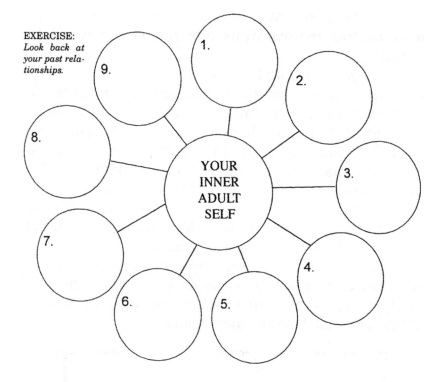

EXERCISE:
*Look back at
your past rela-
tionships.*

YOUR
INNER
ADULT
SELF

1.

2.

3.

4.

5.

6.

7.

8.

9.

Relationship Wheel

EXPLANATION:

If all your partners were like one of your parents, you have found your *type*. You may notice that your Inner Mates alternated between your mother and father. If you switched Adult Role Models from one parent to the other, then you will find two *types* of partners, one like each parent.

Even if you switched Inner Adult Role Models from one relationship to another, the parent you were most like in each relationship is still referred to as your Inner Adult Role Model. Your *fate* is to be like this parent. Remember what Carl Jung believed—that which is hidden deep inside you manifests as *fate*. Your *fate* is the Inner Adult hidden inside of you and the parent you became in your Inner Couple. The other parent, the one your partner behaves most like, is your Inner Mate Model, the *type* of partner to whom you are always attracted.

Once you are aware of the *type(s)* of Inner Mate(s) you subconsciously select, you may want to change your *fate* by changing your own Inner Adult programming, instead of trying to change your Inner Mate(s).

The Rule of Psychogenetics

While your conscious mind is searching for the perfect *MATE,* your subconscious mind is searching for the perfect *MATCH.*

— Anne Teachworth

V. THE REASON

The heart has reasons that reason does not understand.

—Jacques Benigne Bossuet

1. Why We Select or Reject

The series of twists and turns, paths and obstacles, gates and fences that a relationship must maneuver through, over, or around in order for two people to date, marry, and stay together is indeed amazing. People often think they are rejected because they are not good enough, when the real reason their relationships may not have worked is that they were too good. We've mistakenly believed that others who are better looking, richer, smarter, or nicer are more likely to be selected as mates because these traits are supposed to be universally more desirable. Your conscious mind may like those qualities more than others, but your conscious mind is not doing the choosing.

People select or reject a mate based on how similar that person is to their Inner Mate Model and that person's potential for recreating the Inner Couple. Remember, opposites are attracted only if their parents were opposites. If the parents were alike, then two people who are alike will be attracted to each other.

Let's look at some relationships where two people didn't get involved because their histories *couldn't* repeat themselves with each other and their subconscious minds knew it, even if their conscious minds didn't.

Example #1 "What does she have that I don't?" Bambi asked the hypothetical question many a lonely person has posed. The answer, of course, is that Bambi was rejected for being too pretty. Often, it's the so-called positive qualities that don't match the other person's Inner Mate picture. "Bambi's too good looking for my tastes," Derek told his friends. "I just don't feel right around her for some reason."

Given our modern belief systems, it was hard for this beautiful nineteen-year-old model to understand why Derek left her for a quiet, rather plain-looking gal he met at a bookstore. "It was bound to happen," Derek said to her. "We're too different. It wouldn't have worked with you anyhow." Bambi was confused by that statement.

Derek came in to take the Selection Test at Bambi's request. I looked at his Inner Couple programming. Now we had the answer. Bambi was rejected because she didn't match Derek's Inner Mate Model. "My mother wasn't pretty, but she was the most beautiful woman I ever saw. My father was a lucky man. They were like two peas in a pod . . . so much alike. I want a wife like her. They were the happiest couple I ever saw."

Example #2: I knew the minute I looked at Jed's Selection Test that he and Sherri wouldn't make it. I told her what the problems were. Jed came from a set of parents who were opposites and Sherri didn't. Jed's Selection Test showed that his mother was flexible but both his father and stepfather were difficult. In fact, Jed himself told me that no one on his mother's side of the family could put up with either one of her husbands. Jed's mother was his Inner Adult Role Model and he subconsciously chose the same type of troublesome mates she did. Although he didn't like their behaviors, Jed naturally felt more connected to difficult women *or* he automatically became difficult with women who were easy-going in order to get them to be tolerant with him, like his mother was with her mates.

"Now that explains why I feel so irritable and tense

around Jed," Sherri told me when I explained it to her. "He was a real thoughtful guy when I met him, and I was responsive to that. Separately, or on the phone, we're still agreeable, but something strange happens whenever we are together lately. Being around Jed brings out the worst in me.

"Now I understand the musical chairs that are going on. I didn't like feeling that way at all. It's not my usual position. But according to Jed's Inner Couple model, only one of us can end up easy-going like his mother, and he's winning. The only role available for me in a relationship with him is the tense one and I don't want it," Sherri said. "My parents were both small-town, quiet people. So am I. My Inner Adult wants a mutually peaceful relationship when I settle down. My parents are very much alike. Neither one of them are difficult to get along with, either in action or reaction. They are my Inner Couple and I like them a lot better than Jed's Inner Couple. I can smell trouble brewing if I stay with him."

Surprisingly, Jed was in total agreement over what was happening. "Hey, I want to stop doing this, too. I can't tell you how many times I've gotten into this idiotic pattern before Sherri, and it never worked out either way."

EXERCISE:

1 List three things you could do to improve your relationship.
2. List three things you want your partner to do to improve your relationship.
3. List three things your partner wants from you.
4. Are these possibly the same things your parents would have liked from each other?

2. Why Nice Gals Finish Last

Priscilla was just beginning to change her negative relationship pattern when she met Luke at a party.

"I didn't even dare talk to any guys there 'cause I knew I couldn't trust myself to be attracted to a different type yet, but Luke seemed so sincere and genuine, not like the smooth talkers I've been dating. We started out completely infatuated with each other, but it didn't last for him. Once we had sex, he got real busy and would only come over if I called him. I just figured Luke was shy, so I kept calling. But I didn't like running after a man. I got tired real quick of always being the aggressive one. I was used to being pursued by aggressive guys. Having the hots for a man was a new role for me. I needed more reassurance from Luke.

"Unlike my previous relationship partners, Luke never talked about how he felt with me or wanted to see me more than I wanted to see him. He wasn't cold, just cool. I couldn't figure it out until I took the Selection Test. I realized that in all my previous relationships, my quiet, intellectual father had always been my Inner Adult Role Model and my outgoing, attention-demanding mother was my Inner Mate Model. That is, until now. I had switched role models. Luke was acting more like my father, and I was reacting like my mother for the first time in my life. I didn't like it one bit. I wanted him to be more aggressive with me, even though I'd had enough of demanding, possessive men."

Priscilla continued, "I remember how surprised I was to hear from friends that Luke's ex-wife had left him and then bad mouthed him all over town. That seemed strange that she could be so angry at such a shy, sweet guy. He had seemed like such an honorable person to me. The last time I saw Luke, he told me his ex wanted him back and he felt guilty about not wanting to do it.

That didn't make any sense then, but it does now. She was probably a demanding person much like my mother had been with my father, and he was the understanding, compliant partner my father had been."

Her Inner Couple imprint was finally making sense to her.

Priscilla remembered that while she and Luke were still seeing each other, he'd mentioned two other long-term girl friends he'd had who were bitches and always PMSing. They had left him as his ex-wife had. Hearing that had just made Priscilla want to be more understanding with him, not more demanding.

"Luke also told me about his evil sister. It was a tipoff. But I didn't stop to think that it indicated that his sister was like one of his parents and he was like the other. I can only assume how his parents were with each other when he was a child but I think they must have been like mine. He probably had one hot parent and one cool, too."

Love is blind, but hindsight isn't, is it? Priscilla could see their relationship twice as clearly now that Luke's had left her than she could before. It did appear that Luke had her old Inner Couple model. These two matched subconsciously all right . . . in reverse. Without her realizing it, quiet Luke had reminded Priscilla of her father and in response, initially elicited her aggressive mother.

"I should have bitched if I wanted to keep Luke, shouldn't I?" Priscilla said.

Right.

Luke was programmed to bond with an aggressive, selfish partner. Priscilla was continually attracted to men like that before therapy, but would break up with them when they wanted too much of her time.

"This is what Luke was probably starting to feel with me. I stopped calling him, because I realized I hadn't liked anyone imposing on my time that much," she told me in retrospect. "When I went back to being like my Daddy, Luke and I were too much alike, weren't we?"

The problem, exactly. Since both sets of parents were opposites, being with an "alike" partner didn't match either of their Inner Couple patterns. Luke wouldn't have left Priscilla if she'd stayed on her mother's side of her old Inner Couple pattern. You could say Priscilla let Luke down by tolerating his cool behavior the way her father tolerated everything her mother dished out. Priscilla's mother wouldn't have silently put up with Luke's inconsiderateness.

"I'm not switching role models to keep Luke. I'd rather stay single than be a bitch. I want to totally change my Inner Couple, not switch from one extreme to the other."

Priscilla's attraction to Luke demonstrated that she was still drawn to someone with her old couple pattern even though she wanted to break out of it. "I never wanted to be with anyone who was demanding and I sure don't want to be the demanding one, like I was with Luke."

Priscilla was beginning to understand what Psychogenetics is all about, although she was not yet completely free of her attachment to her old pattern. We never had a Selection Test on Luke. I only surmised that he was preconditioned for such a set of opposites, too.

"So I ruined the relationship by staying calm, didn't I?"

Yes, I guess we could say that Priscilla was a disappointment to Luke. Because she was so forward when they first met, he probably thought she could be the aggressive, controlling Inner Mate partner he needed and tell him what to do and where to get off.

Priscilla added, "Now I finally understand why my ex, who used to rant and rave at me all the time, is so very compliant with his new wife. He must have switched to being his opposite parent instead of changing his Inner Couple model. Now his second wife rants and raves at him like he used to do to me when we were married. I love it. Revenge is sweet. We could say she does him to him, so he does me to her. It makes perfect sense."

3. History Repeats Itself

Either by nature or nurture, you, like Priscilla and Luke and the others, repeat not just your parents' unsolved problems but your parents' ineffective coping methods, too. Of course, your parents were simply repeating the post-hypnotic suggestion implanted in their childhoods. They became like their mommies and daddies, and you became like yours. Your parents were your main role models for adulthood. You didn't know them as the people they were outside of their roles. On the Selection Test, the two Adult sections (#2 and #3) ask you to describe your parents as the adults they were and the Parent sections (#4 and #5) ask how they were as parents. Most of you had trouble separating these two descriptions. As children, you were not consciously separating their personality and behaviors into these two categories. You experienced them as one.

Never having been an adult yourself at the time, how your parents were in their adult-adult relationship with their mate (#8), would not have been comprehensible to you in childhood. You may have already been over-whelmed by having to cope with how they were as parents to you. If in childhood your conscious mind was already overloaded by trauma, abuse, fighting, or abandonment, you were especially susceptible to absorbing their Inner Couple model into your subconscious mind and are more likely to still be following its edict.

That is why real conscious choice isn't possible as long as your programmed Inner Adult and Inner Mate remain hidden deep inside your subconscious mind. Books that say you marry someone who represents the parent with whom you have the most unmet needs, miss the subtle but powerful truth: It's not how your mother or father was with you as a child that determines

whom you marry. It's how they were with each other.

Your parents' relationship determines not only whom you pick but whom you become as you move from stage to stage in your relationship journey. The Inner Adult seed that was planted long ago in your childhood will begin to bloom in your adulthood and do its own choosing for you. We all like to think we do the selecting. But from the very first meeting, certain predetermined conditions and traits must be met for the emerging Inner Adult to allow each budding relationship to unfold with a potential mate, or it "dies on the vine."

QUESTIONS:

1. Is this potential mate like one of your parents in any way? Does he or she have same color eyes? Hair? Body build? Voice tonality? Personality type? Behaviors? Postures? Nationality? Accent? Profession? Hobbies? First name? Addictions? Stress reactions? Talents? Weaknesses or strengths? Etc. . . .
2. Are you like the other parent?

4. Adult Child of an Addict

"My mother was cold, critical, and cruel," Tim said. "No matter what I did, she drove me and my Dad nuts trying to please her." As a young child, Tim wanted his co-dependent Adult Role Model father to fix his mother's prescription drug problem. The Inner Child in Tim still had that unmet need to cure his mother. But because of his Inner Adult programming, Tim kept picking women like his mother and got the same disastrous results with each one. All were addicts or alcoholics. His Inner Adult was automatically recreating the original situation and, once again, was unable to fix it. This was most definitely the basic, underlying inner conflict between his Inner Child and his Inner Adult, and it explained the repetitious negative relationships Tim had had.

As an Adult Child of both an addict mother and an enabler father, Tim was the perfect example of a child stuck in an overwhelming situation. No child can fix his mother or father, no matter how hard he tries. "I just wanted to get out of that house as soon as I could," Tim explained. At sixteen, he ran away, determined to have a better life than the one he had endured at home. And he did, until he married a woman much like his mother.

John Bradshaw, author of *Family Secrets, Homecoming*, and other books on the Inner Child, has written extensively over the last few years on the life-long disastrous effect alcoholics, addicts, or abusive parents have on their offspring. All the books say that Adult Children of Alcoholics will usually pick a partner like one of the parents. Bradshaw calls this the family trance. Certainly, trance would explain why Tim picked someone like his mother, a person who couldn't give either him or his father any love or affection. It hadn't made any sense before.

So here, again, was the same question I'd asked myself before with Lisa. Only now I could tell Tim why he'd done the same thing. His Selection Test held the answer for him. But it wasn't Tim's Inner Child who repeatedly picked mates like the mother he wanted nothing more to do with. It was his Inner Adult/self, programmed to pick a mate like the one his Adult Role Model father had, regardless of whether it had been a good choice for his father or would be one for him!

Subconsciously, what had repeated was not just Tim's Inner Adult Role Model parent's choice of a mate, but that Adult Role Model's unmet needs with his mate. It was a double whammy. Both Tim's Inner Adult and Inner Child shared the same unmet need to fix his Inner Mate/parent. Because of it, Tim's subconscious directive to repeat his father's choice of an addict for a mate was twice as strong.

EXERCISE:

1. Look back at your Selection Test. Is your Inner Adult and Inner Mate couple relationship (#8) marked minus (–)?
2. Is your Inner Mate-Inner Child parent-child relationship (#6 or #7) also marked minus (–), as was Tim's?
3. Is your Inner Adult-Inner Child relationship (#6 or #7) marked plus (+) or minus (–)?

5. *Fixing the Past*

I wanted to find some way for Tim to cut loose from his parents' terrible relationship. It was too late to change his childhood—or was it? Tim's unmet need to fix his mother was mainly unfinished Inner Adult business, because his Inner Child had really wanted his passive Adult Role Model father to fix her. In effect, the problem could be handled more effectively as an adult-adult relationship issue, not a parent-child issue, since it had never been the child's job to be a responsible parent to himself in that situation. It was his father's job to protect his son from his mother's cruelty and neglect. What if Tim's father hadn't been so trapped by his own passivity? Would Tim have been different with his own mates? Hadn't Tim just copied his Adult Role Model father's co-dependent behavior in his current relationships?

"But my father never gave up on my Mom," Tim said proudly, giving me some idea of the loyalty he had subconsciously absorbed from observing his father's enabling behavior. But that admiration seemed in direct conflict with Tim's next sentence. "We just did whatever she demanded whenever she got drunk. It was pitiful but it is all I knew to do then and, worse yet, I've gone and done the exact same thing with one wife and two girlfriends since. Something just comes over me and I can't do anything else but put up with their abuse of drugs or me, praying and hoping it'll stop. It didn't. Thank God, they finally left me."

Tim had no mate now. I didn't want him picking another woman like his usual choices. There had to be a way to heal the imprint of his Inner Adult's passivity. Tim didn't have to let go of his Inner Child's need for his father to change his behavior with his mother; he had to accept that his role model father had been without the skill, courage, or programming to do anything different.

I asked Tim if, as a child, he'd ever wished his father had stood up to his mother. "Of course!" he said. I asked him what as a child he had wanted his father to do differently. I had Tim write a new script for them so we could enact his parents' relationship as a stage play, once as it had been and once as he wanted it to be.

"If your father had stopped enabling and demanded she clean up her act, he might have gotten her into treatment and things would have been different at home," I said to Tim. "Then you would not have repeated your father's attitude of putting up with whatever your mate did. You wouldn't have had his passivity modeled into you from the very beginning. Instead, you would have had an assertive Adult Role Model. In fact, you would have brought your father's new effective behavior into your own couple relationships and perhaps wouldn't have been so abused and neglected by the girl-friends you picked."

Tim's eyes lit up. "Maybe I wouldn't even have picked those kind of women in the first place!" he said.

The idea was exciting. We began the process of reimagining and reenacting various scenes of Tim's parents in his past. Maybe we had finally found a way to get history to correct itself instead of repeat itself.

QUESTIONS:

1. What do you like about your partner?
2. What do you dislike?
3. What do you want to change about your partner?
4. What does your partner like about you?
5. What does your partner dislike?
6. What does your partner want to change about you?
7. What did your mother like about your father?
8. What did your father like about your mother?
9. What did your mother dislike about your father?
10. What did your father dislike about your mother?
11. What did your parents want to change about each other?

6. Back Home Again

Lori told us her story. She had just left her latest lover, Mitch, after a two-year live-in relationship.

"I left home to get away from my critical mother, and I'm still trying to get away from her. As I look back on my four relationships, I've picked the same kind of critical mate each time. Mitch was exactly like my mother. The same.

"I've spent ten years in therapy working on my Inner Child's unmet needs with my mother. Now you're telling me I pick partners like her, not because she abused me but because I'm more like my Dad in my adult relationships and he picked an abusive mate. My mother was my Inner Mate Model each time and I didn't even realize it. So all along I should have been working on changing my memory of him so I wouldn't keep picking the same kind of critical mate he did. Help! They all did the same thing that she did once we lived together— insulted and criticized me."

Lori explained that her poor father was always apologizing to her mother for something. "My mother was a constant bitch to both of us. Actually, I used to get beaten because I wouldn't apologize to her like my father did. I didn't have any respect for him because he did that, but as an adult I've been apologizing to Mitch just to keep the peace. Maybe that is why my dad did it, too. I guess I ought to pick a mate who is more like my father from now on, right?"

Well, not yet. Then she would become like her mother and abuse him. It was her Inner Couple blueprint that needed to be changed.

7. *What Do You Do When You Don't Know What to Do?*

The two greatest fears an infant has are the fear of falling and the fear of loud noises. Good parents are supposed to protect, nurture, support, and keep their young children in a safe environment during their early years. It is, however, a sad fact that for too many children, the scariest sights and sounds happen at home. Parents who are abusive to each other or their children imprint terrors, which stay with them throughout their lives and show up when the children themselves become parents. But that's a complicated issue which is beyond the scope of what we're exploring in this book and will be dealt with in the next.

Here I want to deal mainly with the effect that fighting parents have on the Inner Couple imprint you got as a child. Mom and Dad's angry relationship certainly would have produced pain, terror, and loud noises, not only for them, but for you, too. Often, the young child grows up in a war zone. The parents' example implants the original idea that continual fighting is the way an adult-to-adult relationship is. What gets recorded in your Inner Adult is that love means terror, love means rage, love means neglect, and so on. When your mating process begins, the pull of that old post-hypnotic suggestion compels you to do the same thing in your adulthood that your Inner Adult Role Model did with your Inner Mate Model parent.

The Cycle of Abuse repeats itself under stress because those behaviors are on automatic. Even if you consciously don't want to do what they did, you are conditioned to do what you know how to do. Remember, an adult's greatest fear is the fear of the unknown. Although you may consciously want to handle a current stressful situation differently, under the stress of it, your subconscious flashes a familiar picture of what your Inner Adult parent did in the same situation, and you regress to that programmed reaction from your parents. It is the pull of the familiar. Under pressure, it's hard to even think of doing anything other than what they did. Your conscious mind is no longer in charge of your Inner Adult behavior. Under stress, your Adult Role Model parent of the past takes over. It's conditioning. **Remember, any important change in your life is a stress.**

Over and over, that old familiar reaction to stress keeps you from doing anything other than what that Adult Role Model did in your past. You feel helpless under stress because your subconscious mind has no other programmed responses or solutions. Under stress, you cannot think clearly or rationally, and in order to avoid the anxiety of not knowing what to do, you quickly resort to imprinted behaviors that your parents taught you.

Some of the most common stresses in adulthood are:
— being angry, alone, bored, confused, hurried, infatuated, intimidated, passionate.
— death of a loved one, sickness of self or loved one.
— getting drunk, fired, hired, laid off, married, or divorced.
— moving to a new town, office, or home.
— changing your lifestyle, up or down, with or without a partner.
— feeling overwhelmed, overworked, scared, sad, tired, or tense.
— having sex, money, or relationship problems.

If your Adult Role Model parents were abusive, either to you or to each other, their behavior nevertheless provided you with a familiar way of dealing with new or stressful situations. Under stress, you do what they did, even if they told you not to repeat their mistakes—even if you swore you'd never be like them.

The only solution to stress that you learned subconsciously is *their* behavior. It's an automatic reflex to react their way. The Cycle of Abuse comes from negative role models. If you had had two positive role models and a positive Inner Couple imprint, the Cycle of Happiness would automatically repeat itself in your life.

It was certainly more than mere coincidence that under stress Bill Clinton was drawn to Monica, a young woman who was a replica of both his mother and grandmother in his first ten years of life. As a result of stresses on all sides, Clinton had unconsciously regressed to this latent Inner Mate pattern from childhood. The Inner Couple scene was set. Monica was already working near the President, not only flirting with him, but aggressive in her adoration of him. He may not have even consciously noted that she also looked much like his mother had when he was a young child, or that she was acting with him the same way he'd often seen both his mother and grandmother acting with the men in town. Even his mother's history of falling in love with his father at first sight was part of the Inner Couple trance he was obviously acting out.

To add even more fuel to the fire, the twenty-one year old student/intern's pursuit of this much older man in the White House where she worked, repeated the history of Clinton's mother falling in love with his much older father when she first met him in the emergency room where she worked as a student/nurse many years before. Monica matched Bill's earliest Inner Couple program to a T, and as a result, he automatically responded with both fathers' (his Inner Adults) womanizing behaviors toward her. Since Bill never knew his real father, his relationship with Monica Lewinsky certainly makes a case for inherited personality predisposition.

8. *The Power of Having Emotional Precedents*

Under stress, we all regress. Regression means a return to a state of mind or behaviors of a earlier age, and usually behavior that was familiar in childhood. Stress produces transference and brings up reactions that originated in another time with another person, usually a parent role model from childhood.

People under stress don't see or hear their current partner. They react the same way their Inner Adult parent did on similar occasions and treat their current partner the same way their role model treated the Inner Mate parent. All stress reactions will be based on that early childhood reality, which was established in their family-of-origin. The Inner Adult Role Model imprint has remained as the first response simply because it is the only imprinted stress reaction in the subconscious memory.

Several points are important here:

1. Emotional precedent identifies what, where, and to whom we return. What we have come to identify as our Inner Couple will surface under interactional stress. Under stress, what pops up in our mind's eye is the same interactional dialogue they used, with its programmed set of cues and responses, early emotional interactional patterns, and learned role model expectations of self and others. That is an emotional precedent.

2. Our familiar reaction patterns from childhood are referred to as our second nature, but really they're our first nature. They're what come naturally. Second nature is what comes out automatically, without having to think about it first or decide what to say or do. It's familiar. But just because it is familiar, does not mean it is comfortable.

3. Consistently, people will repeat familiar behaviors rather than change to something unfa-

miliar, even if the unfamiliar is a lot more comfortable. Often, the familiar is indeed highly uncomfortable . . . or painful, or unsatisfying, or problematic. Why would we want to keep on doing it then? Because we are in a trance. The repetitive examples from our parents have all the properties of post-hypnotic suggestion. They are the only behavioral responses we have in our subconscious memory. Under stress, we will regress to the familiar, and what is most familiar is what we were taught through our parents' repeated examples in our childhood.

4. Psychogenetics recognizes the need to establish new and positive emotional precedents in our Inner Couple programming to provide an alternative subconscious reaction. If you are to avoid immediately reacting to stressful cues with the same imprinted negative response your parents used, you must have alternate positive responses programmed into your subconscious memory. It is not reasonable to think a hypnotized subject can consciously choose to suppress the subconscious negative suggestion while caught in a trance. The conscious mind is not in charge at such times.

5. To reprogram the Inner Adult, we must first bring that imprinted behavior into conscious awareness *before* **the stress situation reoccurs, and then install another solution in which all participants in the family-of-origin have a positive emotional and behavioral experience.** Only if this new outcome is integrated into childhood memories prior to the stimulus situation, can we change the previously imprinted behavior and establish a positive precedent for the current relationship to follow when the same environmental stress presents itself again.

6. Roleplaying our Inner Couple of the past is necessary to access the old subconscious imprint and program a new, positive stimulus-response pattern.

QUESTIONS:

1. What did your mother do in your childhood when she got stressed?
2. What did your father do when your mother got stressed?
3. What did your father do in your childhood when he got stressed?
4. What did your mother do when your father got stressed?
5. What do you do now when you get stressed?
6. What does your partner usually do when you get stressed? What did your former partners do?
7. What does your partner usually do when he or she gets stressed? What did your former partners do?
8. What do you do now when your partner gets stressed?
9. What would you like your partner to do?
10. What would your partner like you to do?
11. What would you like to do differently under stress now?
12. What would you have liked your mother to do differently when she got stressed in your childhood?
13. What would you have liked your father to do differently when he got stressed in your childhood?
14. How would you be different now if they had improved their stress reactions then?
15. How will your children be different if you improve your stress reaction now?

9. Quack, Quack, Quack

You have only to see a stage hypnotist at work to understand that people who are hypnotized are not in their normal, wide-awake, conscious adult minds. These subjects usually exhibit a dazed stare while being obviously transfixed by the hypnotist's voice, pendulum, or eyes. Seemingly unaware of the other people in the room, they respond only to the hypnotist's commands and comply with them easily and effortlessly.

I will give you a typical example.

"Be a duck," the hypnotist says.

Immediately, the woman on stage quacks like a duck, showing no inhibitions despite the audience watching her, nor does she respond to their laughter, which is clearly audible. There is no stress for her, because her conscious mind is asleep when she is in trance. We could say she is regressed to a state of subconsciousness while hypnotized.

The hypnotist tells her she will awaken in one minute feeling fully refreshed and alert; her conscious mind will not remember what has happened on stage, but he has also implanted a post-hypnotic suggestion by telling her that anytime she heard the word *duck* after returning to her seat, she will stand up in the audience and begin to quack out loud. The post-hypnotic suggestion will keep her quacking until the hypnotist says, "Stop!"

"Is that understood?" the hypnotist asks her while she is still in trance.

"Yes," the subject replies.

"Wake up," the hypnotist commands, and it appears that the trance has been lifted.

The subject returns to her seat in the audience. We think she has returned to her former self, but she has not. Unknown to her conscious self, the post-hypnotic suggestion lies latent in her subconscious mind, awaiting the stimulus.

"How was it?" her friends in the audience will ask, giggling over the quacking of which the subject has no recollection.

"Oh, fine," she'll say, because her conscious mind remembers nothing of what went on in the trance state on stage.

However, five minutes later, as the stage hypnotist tells the audience a joke about duck hunting, she is immediately regressed to the subconscious state, and, without consciously deciding to do so, promptly stands and begins to quack. Unaware of his prior hypnotic suggestion, she is puzzled by her own actions and confused as to why she is doing this. However, in spite of the stress of the conflict between her conscious and subconscious minds, she is unable to stop. In fact, the stress regresses her even more. Now thoroughly embarrassed by her own behavior, which was clearly out of her control, she is neither able to explain her behavior nor stop her response if the stimulus is repeated. Not until the hypnotist says "stop" is she able to sit down and be quiet.

Her friends explain to her that she was hypnotized on stage and commanded to quack like that, but their explanation is a surprise to her since her conscious mind still doesn't remember what happened on stage. Her conscious mind wasn't awake on stage and didn't hear any of that. Her subconscious mind was the only part of her that heard the post-hypnotic command. Her conscious mind woke up when she left the stage and stayed in charge until the hypnotist said the word *duck* again. At that point, her subconscious mind took over in order to carry out its programmed response to the stimulus.

Because the command was implanted in the subject's subconscious mind, her conscious mind had no control over her response. Her body was awake, but her behavior was under the spell of the hypnotist. The hypnotized subject is not in control. She cannot remember the induction, much less the instruction to quack, either the first time or the second, and no amount of explaining what happened on stage will make sense to her. It was her subconscious mind, that sleeping giant that wakes up at night and in dreams—that master computer that controls her heart and respiration—that followed the hypnotist's instructions. Her conscious mind—her ego, her own decision maker—was asleep, in a trance, out of the way, or under the spell of an authority, and definitely not in charge of the human being that it pretends to control.

The conscious mind is the less powerful of the two minds, but its ego is certainly the more arrogant. When asked a question that it does not know how to answer, the ego often says "It's not important," or "I forgot." Often the reason it forgot is even forgotten, but it won't tell you that. Your ego keeps secrets from you when it no longer wants you to remember the stimulus situation. Denial is the means the conscious mind has at its "disposal" to rid its memory of information that is painful, confusing, embarrassing, or otherwise best left unnoticed. Some of the events in childhood certainly fall in that category, and for that very reason are stored away in your subconscious mind right now, hidden deep inside.

Most of us are aware of the difficulty we have remembering what happened in our early childhood—from birth to about five years of age—but that is exactly the time when most of our programming occurred. We remember more events after five years of age than before.

None of us consciously remember learning to speak the same language our parents spoke, but we did. We learned how to walk and eat with a spoon like they did. We learned not what made sense to us, but what made sense to them. All the examples from our childhood were recorded in our subconscious, but not consciously remembered because they were just the way it was. Add to that, the many experiences we wanted to forget or the ones we didn't understand. We remember some things about childhood, but only vaguely. What was hypnotized into us as children, we don't remember learning at all even though we often repeat those behaviors automatically in adulthood. They operate like post-hypnotic suggestions.

Therapists frequently use hypnosis for age regression, which simply means that the minds of clients in trance are focused more in a past time than in the present. This type of therapeutic hypnosis can recover not only the lost memories but post-hypnotic suggestions from childhood, and as you will soon see it, can also be used to create positive precedents.

10. Pushing Each Other's Buttons

Couples are always pushing each other's buttons and getting trance reactions from childhood. What we don't often realize is that every button that gets pushed brings up a previous negative post-hypnotic reaction still lodged inside you or your partner's subconscious Inner Couple. Either the original pair bond situation is still unfinished or it's still painful.

Newton's Third Law of Motion states that "For every action there is an equal and opposite reaction." The rule in Psychogenetics is similar: "For every reaction, there was an equal or opposite action." In essence, cues and responses are sets of familiar communication pairs. It's important to know that any reaction one has to the other's cue is usually a repeat of a parent or alternate role model's response. If there were no similar unresolved situations in the Inner Couples, there would be no automatic negative reactions to the same stimulus in the present couple.

Couples always think it's their current partner who is making them feel bad by pushing their buttons on purpose. They want their partner to stop making them feel bad. Rarely do they realize how they themselves are locked into maintaining the previous generation's automatic reaction. **Becoming aware that the original stimulus for your response happened in your parents' relationship is the first step to coming out of trance.**

The good news is you are now in charge of the Inner Adult's attitude. It's your post-hypnotic suggestion that's got to be changed and you're just the person to do it. The bad news is that nobody in the present can stop your quacking except your own Inner Adult's role model. That is the one who has to stop first. But you don't have to wait for that parent to change before you can come out of trance. You don't have to be stuck with how your Adult Role Model hypnotized you.You can change your subconscious memories of that parent and act differently toward your partner.

Your difficulty with your partner simply provides you with the opportunity to access your Inner Couple pattern and re-solve the unfinished business of your parents' relationship. It's easy to see where your partner should change his or her behavior, but unfortunately, your partner has that same wish about you, too. Wanting your partner to change according to your plan is not the solution here. Most partners want their partner to change in exactly the same way their Inner Adult Role Model parents wanted their Inner Mate Model parents to change. In order for couples to evolve, they have to leave their parents' historic stimulus/response patterns behind, go into the unknown and change themselves the way they wanted their Inner Adult parent to change. Then, and only then, will the Inner Couple begin to evolve instead of revolve!

In order to accomplish this, reprogramming must start one generation below the surface of the couple's current behavior. In the sessions I conduct, we first access, and then reassociate, each client to his or her Adult and Mate role models. This is accomplished by reenacting the way the client's parents related to each other during the client's childhood. We use three chairs for this exercise, one each to represent the mother, the father, and the Inner Child. As the client occupies each chair in turn, he or she identifies the person represented by describing the way that person looked in the past, then acting the way that person did then.

This Psychogenetic method goes right to the heart of the unresolved issues between the parents, which have been blocked from awareness. Usually those issues are reflected in the minuses placed on the Selection Test. Go

back to the Childhood History Chart and remind yourself of where those are on your test. These identify the
people and patterns you need to reprogram.

Listen to Rosemary's story:

"My mother was always mad at my father. Just like
her, I have been angry and on edge ever since Lester
and I got our own apartment. I really don't want to be
like this. I don't know what has come over me. It's as if
I'm possessed by some demonic force. Why on earth am
I reacting like this? I really love Lester. He is so sweet
and loving to me."

I had Rosemary read her mother's traits out loud so
she could realize that these Inner Adult's traits also
described her now. When she first came in, she could
only see Lester's faults were like her father's had been.
Becoming aware that she was the same kind of wife her
mother had been was the first step in coming out of her
Inner Adult trance.

The post-hypnotic suggestion was no longer hiding
deep in Rosemary's subconscious and could not control
her once she became consciously aware of this similarity to her mother's traits and behaviors. The next time
a stressful situation occurred, Rosemary might have a
conscious choice and be able to act in ways other than
her mother's impulsive, automatic, imprinted reactions
to her mate. Until we brought her trance into con-
sciousness, Rosemary had been reacting like her mother
would, instead of how she wanted herself to react. Now,
she was changing her response by changing her
mother's.

Rosemary and Lester had rehearsed their roles in
childhood when they played mommies and daddies. Just
like actors in a play that had been running on
Broadway for twenty-five years, they had fallen into
reciting their memorized set of cues and responses. Not
until one of them changed his or her own lines and sent
another cue would the automatic response be different.

The cast might have changed over the years, but Acts I, II, and III of the Inner Couple play would be the same unless they were rewritten. The couple would meet, fall in love, and the drama unfold . . . yet again.

QUESTIONS:
1. What is the title of your parents' play? And yours?
2. Is it a one act play? How long does it last?
3. What happens in Act I, II, and III in your reruns?
4. How would you like the lines rewritten? The ending?

11. Never Too Late to Have a Happy Marriage

Betty and Nolan were another example of two people who met, fell in love, married, and much to their disappointment did not live happily ever after. Together for ten years when they first came to see me, they were in their late twenties, had two young sons, and were on the verge of divorce. Betty arrived for counseling confused about what to do. She was thinking about having an affair and perhaps leaving Nolan. I began by giving her the Selection Test, which elicited the origins of Betty's problematic relationship behavior in her parents' marriage. Looking at it, I was able to quickly identify the inherited unresolved problems that were being repeated in Betty's marriage to Nolan. She was like her father.

Remember, the Psychogenetics Model I applied here is personality bound, not gender bound. The Selection Test clarified which parent Betty had identified with as her relationship role model, the person whose manner of being and interacting with a mate she had copied.

Much to her dismay, Betty was able to see the similarity of her potentially unfaithful behavior with Nolan to her hated father's sexually abusive behaviors to her mother. "Nolan acts just exactly like my sweetheart of a mother did with my father. I hated the way she put up with everything he did and all his 'women friends.' I swore I'd never let a man treat me the way my mother let my father treat her. I guess in some strange way, I really kept that promise to myself, didn't I?"

Notice that Betty's father is her Inner Adult Role Model, not the stereotypical same-sex parent, as was previously assumed to be the case. Even though Betty's mother was her favorite parent, she was not her favorite adult. Nor was her mother Betty's Inner Adult Role Model on a subconscious level. Her mother was her

Inner Mate Model. Nolan was more like her mother as an adult than Betty was. Betty took after her father, and because she hated him, she had now begun to hate herself.

Using this Psychogenetic analysis, we focused first on the similar interactions Betty and her father had with their respective mates. It was most important that Betty roleplay the unhappy interactions in her mother and father's husband-wife relationship. I had her write some new memories and prepare to enact a new Inner Couple script. Reprogramming Betty's parents' adult-adult relationship was definitely more effective as a corrective approach than the traditional therapy methods of working on either Betty's unhappy adult-adult relationship with Nolan or Betty's neglectful parent-child relationship with her father.

The fixed pattern that was damaging Betty and Nolan's relationship was Betty's own subconscious repetition of her abusive father's treatment of his mate that was motivating Betty's abusive treatment of hers. If Betty could change her prior generation's adult-adult model in her Inner Couple programming, she could produce a new automatic positive response to her Inner Mate, Nolan. Roleplaying positive fictional dialogues between her parents would give Betty some prior memory of her parents working through the stuck places in their relationship and make it possible for her to try these positive new behaviors with Nolan.

After one thousand case studies using this Psychogenetic method, I now consider the unsolved problems from the parents' relationships to be the most relevant therapeutic restructuring work for a client with a couple relationship problem. My emphasis in this Psychogenetic model of couple counseling is not the interaction between the current couple but its similarity to deeper problematic couple interactions inherited from previous generations. As a therapist, my initial intervention is therefore directly into the parents' relationship in the past, rather than into the couple's relationship in the present.

EXERCISE:

1. Pretend for a moment that you are your Mate Model parent. Imagine what it was like for that parent to have a relationship with your Adult Role Model parent.
2. Then imagine telling that Adult Role Model parent how you feel about yourself in a relationship with him/her and how you feel about yourself away from him/her.
3. What would you say about your mate to other people?
4. How does your present relationship with your mate resemble your parents' relationship with each other back then?

12. Reprogramming Exercise

Let's use Betty's work as an example for you to follow. We began with a systematic reenactment of Betty's parents' husband-wife imprinted interactional pattern. Betty first roleplayed herself as a child watching her parents' relationship; second, her mother interacting with her father; and third, her father interacting with her mother.

We set up the three chairs to represent the original family triad. Sitting in the Inner Child chair, Betty remembered several unpleasant scenes between her parents and roleplayed each of them in first person, present tense, as they had been when she was a child. Sitting in her mother's chair, she introduced herself as young Inez (Betty's mother), spoke as Inez in her twenties, and told us about her husband Pedro (Betty's father), whom she (Inez) loved very much. Next Betty sat in her father's chair, introduced herself as if she were Pedro, and told us about his relationship with Inez, who was always nagging him to stay home more and spend time with her and the kids. Then Betty re-created a typical dialogue between her parents while moving back and forth between their two chairs.

Roleplaying each parent like this generated a wealth of previously forgotten feeling-memories that had been unavailable to Betty when she was only sitting in the child chair, pretending to watch her parents. It also clarified for Betty the difference between her parents as adults in their relationship with each other then, and her limited view of them only as parents to her.

"I'd honestly never thought about either of my parents as people with a childhood or life before they met each other. They were just my parents until I did the three-chair roleplay," Betty said. It was obvious her Inner Child's confusion had cleared up considerably during this exercise. She began to see them as real people.

Returning to the child chair, Betty told both of her parents how she wished they would have been with each other. Then she again roleplayed her mother and father interacting, only this time as the adults she had wanted them to be. We took several negative memories and roleplayed each one, once as it had been and then once as she wanted it to be. After restructuring several of her negative Inner Couple experiences, Betty returned to her Inner Child chair to assimilate these new positive conversations into her childhood memory. She eagerly watched, listened, and felt their new-found contentment as she remembered her parents finally solving their unresolved issues.

These roleplaying sessions presented Betty with positive solutions and new interactional behaviors to apply in her current adult-adult relationship with her husband, Nolan. Over a period of ten sessions, roleplaying several more childhood adult-adult experiences, Betty was able to replace her negative Inner Couple programming with a positive relationship model. In one session she roleplayed her father as he told her mother how much he needed her to take care of him, the children, and the home. "It was the first time I'd ever heard my father say one nice thing to my mother." It made Betty (as Inez) cry for joy.

The next session Betty told me with amazement how excited Nolan had gotten when she told him how much she needed him. "Not in all the years I have been married, has it ever occurred to me to let Nolan know how much I appreciated him. I thought he already knew that, after all he does for me around the house. Nor had I ever before seen my father do that with my mother. Not one word of kindness. It would have made so much difference to my mother had he given her some loving attention. You know, after twelve years of his abuse, and no affection, my mother finally left my father. And my father spent the next twenty years of his life trying to get her to take him back. I guess that's where Nolan and I were headed. He said he was about to give up trying to get some positive attention from me. I'm glad we took an alternative route. I mean, I'm glad we built an alternative route to take. It would have been so much easier if I'd had positive role models to start with. But I have them inside me now."

EXERCISE:

1. Write down how you would have wanted your parents to change or fix their relationship. Who would you have wanted to do what? How would the other parent respond differently? Roleplay them doing that.
2. Then write the story as if it had really happened that way in your childhood, adding in the details of the room they were in, what year and time of day it was, the age you were then, and how your parents looked as they related to each other the new way.
3. Retell the story from memory out loud. If possible, use a tape recorder so you can play it back over and over again.
4. Listen to the taped account several times each week, preferably at bedtime, so it can go into your subconscious mind as you fall asleep and gradually become the basis for your new dream relationship.

VI. THE HISTORY

History repeats itself, and that's one of the things that's wrong with history.
—Clarence Darrow

1. The Family Drama

In childhood and adolescence, we are playing mommies and daddies and practicing for our lead roles when we grow up. From birth to twelve years of age, we are physically and emotionally dependent and therefore highly suggestible. In our teens, our Inner Child begins to fade into our subconscious and our Inner Adult programming begins to emerge. The conflict between our Inner Child and our emerging Inner Adult is visibly obvious in the changes we undergo in both body and mind. As teenagers approaching adulthood, even though we may let go of our parents as our conscious role models, they remain our subconscious role models. Now it is our peers who have become increasingly important. The mating process has begun. Since none of us knew our parents before they were parents, we are usually more program-free in Act I, before we start the mating process, than afterwards.

Before we fall in love or get sexually involved with someone, we are much more in our Inner Child role than we ever will be again with that person. People are different after they fall in love because their Inner Adult has surfaced in their personality. Once the mating process begins, we are inclined to automatically act like our Inner Adult Role Model parent, even though we weren't anywhere around to watch his or her mating behavior unfold. The moment we start auditioning

146

potential partners for the Inner Mate role, our Inner Couple program gets activated. Unless the lines are interrupted or rewritten, we are headed for full couple trance in Act III, when we ourselves become parents. Remember, the Inner Couple has its own script and your Inner Adult knows your part by heart. Most people still remember their "first love." That experience marks their first transition from Inner Child to Inner Adult and, because it is the first, forms a lasting imprint in the heart.

Just like our native language, and the post-hypnotic suggestion to quack, the cues and responses learned from our parents surface then in our personalities without our consciously desiring them to do so.

Most of you do not notice the changes from Act I to Act III in yourself, only in your partner. Your role is that familiar to you. You've seen and heard it before in your Adult Role Model parent. As your relationship progresses, you become more like your Adult Role Model was with his or her mate. Even though you may not notice your changes, your partner will. The fact is that what you do and say will seem normal to you. As you move from meeting to dating to sex, your lines are becoming more rehearsed. You are getting into your part and auditioning partners for the other lead role in the Inner Couple. As the curtain goes down on the first act, the two of you may be feeling fairly secure because you have made it this far.

In Act II, as a new couple you are preparing to live together or get married. Now, both of you are trying your best to play the parts of the original leads you remember from childhood. As the plot thickens, both of you display other parts of your parents' personalities that your partner didn't see at first glance or that you didn't even know were hiding inside you. In other words, under stress (and any new situation or change is a stress), your parents will show up inside of you, while your partner's parents are showing up in her or him. Your Inner Adult Role Models are now both starring in and directing your Inner Couple play and making sure that the familiar cues and responses stay the same. I call this quacking. Often, the person auditioning for the role of your Inner Mate is not right for the part and the relationship can go no further than Act I or II. (They can't play mommies and daddies right.)

"Ten years ago when Harry decided not to leave his wife and marry me, I thought I would die. The agony of the loss of my dream was so intense and physically painful, I never expected to recover. It took me five years," Jan said, recalling their tragic breakup.

As a therapist, I'd always thought the pain Jan felt when Harry broke up with her was the pain she had felt as a child when her father left. Now I know it was the pain her Inner Adult Role Model mother felt when Jan's father ended their relationship. Over a decade later, with the help of Psychogenetics, Jan roleplayed, released her mother's grief, and finally understood what had happened.

"Harry and I have a loving long distance friendship now. Just like our song, he *just calls to say I love you*. He says I am in his thoughts every day and always with him. On my answering machine, he tells me how precious I am to him. The other day, I called to thank him for his latest expression of love. I'm long over the dream of marrying him but still somewhat curious about what happened that ended our affair. I asked him why he has so much resistance to being with me when he is so unhappy with his wife and she with him. 'I don't have any resistance to you,' he says. 'It's to us being married. We don't fit.'

"Given the information of the Selection Test," Jan continued, "that statement now makes perfect sense to me. Harry's picture of a married couple's relationship does not fit what happened between us. We love each other too much. That intense passion between us doesn't match his Inner Adult and Inner Mate programming, or mine—neglecting me does! We had the most wonderful love affair either of us ever had or ever expect to have again. But that's as far as it could go. Neither of us is programmed to get the love we want, only to have the longing for it.

"Now I know why our relationship fizzled out right at the moment he wanted to marry me. Harry told me how unhappy his parents were all their lives together, but they never split up. He takes great pride in the fact that his father stayed with his mother even though his father had many affairs and his mother was constantly jealous. I have come to realize that if Harry and I had married, he would still be having affairs and I would be jealous, too, like his wife was of me and his mother was with his father. I can't change him. There are only two people in this world I can change—me and my memory of my mother. That way, I won't get involved with an unavailable man again the way she did."

EXERCISE:

1. Look back at your past relationships (on the Relationship Wheel at the end of Chapter IV). At which stage did the trouble start? And end?
2. At which stage did the relationship end? Or at which stage did the trouble get resolved?
3. How are your past relationships like those of your parents'?

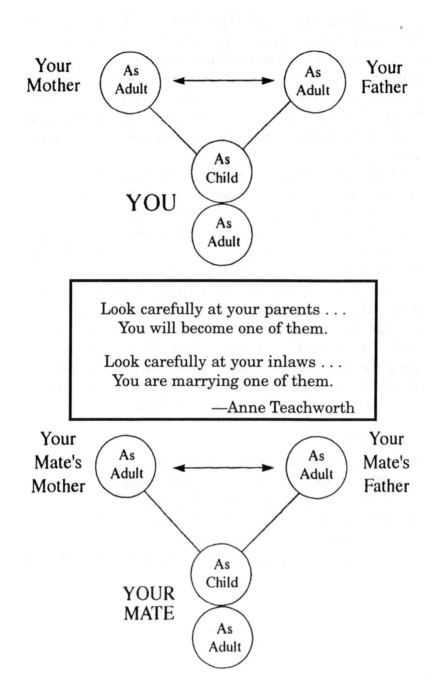

Your
Mother

As
Adult

As
Adult

Your
Father

As
Child

YOU

As
Adult

Look carefully at your parents . . .
You will become one of them.

Look carefully at your inlaws . . .
You are marrying one of them.

—Anne Teachworth

Your
Mate's
Mother

As
Adult

As
Adult

Your
Mate's
Father

As
Child

YOUR
MATE

As
Adult

Relationship Imprints

2. That Old Familiar Feeling

The magnetic attraction you feel today towards someone when you fall in love is the same feeling that existed between your parents in their attraction and mating period. That feeling is the spell that was cast in your early childhood environment by your relationship Mate Models. It's what they felt for each other then. The memory of that feeling is synonymous with falling in love for you. The emotional energy that existed between your parents when they first met is the feeling that your Inner Adult recognizes as important at the beginning stage of your relationship. Be it joy, fear, passion, love, anger, or fun, it is the chemistry between you.

What happens between two people who connect positively or negatively is just a replay of that old familiar feeling between their parents. It calls to them again and again, generation to generation.

Example #1: "In my first marriage, my wife was fooling around a lot. I was so jealous it made me sick. I lost weight, cried a lot, and it still hurts to think about her with some other guy. I got very depressed after the divorce. I promised myself I wouldn't get in that situation again, and here I am back in the same boat with my second wife, Sylvia. I was so attracted to Sylvia when we met. I asked her to marry me on the third date. She was cool, but she said yes because I could give her a lot of financial security like her mother's second husband had when Sylvia was a child and her father left them."

If Mark and Sylvia had taken the Selection Test before they married, Mark would have realized that Sylvia's Adult Role Model was her father, and even though she hated him for leaving her mother (her favorite parent), Sylvia was programmed to do the same to Mark.

"Last week I asked Sylvia if she was seeing someone

else. I should have asked her if she was *being* someone else—like her father. She said she wasn't having an affair, but I don't believe her. Or rather, I don't trust myself when I believe her. I thought I knew my first wife better than that, too. Sylvia goes on trips with her girlfriends. They last too long for me!

"One of the similarities between my first and second marriages is that we now sleep in separate rooms. Sylvia and I haven't had sex in months. My first wife was having sex with other people. I still feel stupid for trusting her. I didn't find out she was fooling around the whole time we were married, until after the divorce. Everybody else knew but me. I was the last person to find out. They all knew but didn't want to hurt me. I think that's happening again," Mark said.

"Why don't I kick Sylvia out? What's keeping me in this? I don't know. Maybe I'm stuck in that familiar feeling we talked about . . . distrust. I don't know if I'm suspicious or naive. I want to trust Sylvia. I can't be constantly worried if she is doing something behind my back. My mother was worried about my father all my life," Mark said. "Both my wives are strong, independent, professional woman. Both are very attractive, and have outgoing personalities. Both are like my Dad, now that I think about it. Wow, I never realized that before! I loved my father, but he gave my mother one hell of a time. I wonder now if he was fooling around with someone else."

Example #2: Lana regretted divorcing Barry almost as much as she regretted marrying him. "My mother regretted marrying my father and then regretted not having the courage to divorce him. My father regretted not leaving my mother. I don't have to be a rocket scientist to see the familiar feeling here is regret. Maybe I should change that, or live to regret it," Lana mused.

EXERCISE:

1. Below and on the following page, underline the feelings that describe how you felt or behaved with each of your partners when you first met them and/or how you feel or behave now.
2. Below, and on the following page, circle the feelings that describe how each of your partners felt about you or behaved when you first met and/or how they feel and behave now.
3. What are the five most frequent feelings you have in a relationship? Place a check mark by them.
4. Notice the similarities as these relationships progressed.
5. What feeling do you usually end up having?

Addicted	Content
Admired	Controlled
Afraid	Controlling
Alcoholic	Crazy
Alive	Creative
Amused	Critical
Angry	Cruel
Anxious	Daring
Apologetic	Delighted
Appreciated	Dependent
Asexual	Depressed
Ashamed	Discouraged
Bewildered	Distant
Bored	Distrustful
Cheating	Dumbfounded
Cheerful	Embarrassed
Concerned	Empty
Confident	Encouraged
Confused	Energetic

Excited

Extravagant

Faithful

Fascinated

Flirty

Foolish

Friendly

Frightened

Frustrated

Furious

Guilty

Happy

Hateful

Helpless

Hopeful

Hostile

Humorous

Hurt

Ignored

Important

Inadequate

Infatuated

Inferior

Insecure

Insignificant

Interested

Interesting

Intimate

Intimidated

Invaded

Involved

Irresponsible

Irritated

Jealous

Joyful

Lonely

Loved

Loving

Lying

Mad

Mean

Miserable

Mystified

Nurturing

Obligated

Paranoid

Passionate

Peaceful

Pensive

Playful

Possessed

Possessive

Powerful

Protective

Protected

Proud

Raging

Rebellious

Recognized

Regretful

Rejected

Relaxed

Resentful

Respected

Responsible

Responsive

Sad

Safe

Satisfied

Scared

Seduced

Selfish

Sentimental

Sensitive

Serene

Sexual

Sexy

Shamed

Shy

Smart

Spiritual

Stimulated

Stupid

Submissive

Superior

Tense

Thankful

Thoughtful

Tired

Trapped

Trusting

Valuable

Validated

Weak

Wimpy

Worried

Worthwhile

(Any others?)

3. Under the Spell

It is more than coincidence that many people tend to be drawn to a mate who has a set of pair bonds similar to their own parents, and a similar history.

Obviously, one of the subconscious imperatives Harry and Jan had followed was to find a partner who could recreate the emotional environment of their parents' relationships, and who could do that better than a partner who had shared a similar parental history? A new partner only matches such requirements up to a certain point but not past it. Both partners must have the same relationship instructions and be able to recreate the same familiar Inner Couple feeling in order to move to the next stage of the relationship. When they do, it's because both sets of parents were similar. Harry's and Jan's were not.

Jan's role model had actually left her husband. Harry's mother had not. In Ashley and Joe's case, both parental sets had remained married.

"If I searched the world over, I couldn't find anyone more like my father than Joe, my first husband. The battling between us was just like my parents. I was always scared of my father when he was drunk. My mother left him several times but kept going back. Why on earth I would be fascinated by a man like him, I'll never know. But in all honesty, I didn't think Joe was like that when I met him. He changed after we were married and became just like his father, too. I married him because he had always said he didn't like the way his parents acted toward each other. His father hit his mother all the time but she never left, either. You'd think he wouldn't do the very same things he hated in his father, but he does! He's always sorry after he hits me. I try to forgive him cause it's the right thing to do. I don't want to break up my marriage. We both want this to work."

Given that we now understand that partners are picked to recreate the interaction between the original pair bonds in the family of origin, we must now take a look at the magnetic energy that attracts these two types of people to each other. Let's take a look at the power of emotion. That's E for energy . . . energy in motion. It's *e-motion* that is the subject of those love songs.

Whatever emotion existed between your mother and father at each succeeding stage of their relationship, is the feeling your Inner Couple programming seeks to recreate for you. Your Inner Adult and your Inner Mate are drawn to each other and held together by the same feeling that was present in your parents' relationship. **You and your partner will stay connected as long as you both continue to repeat the same behaviors that were imprinted in your mind's eye. If either one stops the familiar set of cues and/or responses, you will begin to disconnect emotionally from your Inner Couple programming and have an opportunity to either re-solve or evolve the relationship.**

QUESTION:
1. What is the feeling that existed between you and your partner when you first met?
2. When you first got together as a couple?
3. What is the feeling that exists between you and your mate now in your relationship?
4. What is the feeling that holds you and your mate together?
5. What was the feeling between your mother and your father when you were a child?
6. What is the feeling you most often associate with love?

4. Too Close for Comfort

"Foster and I had decided not to see each other anymore after he moved out," Nancy told me. A year ago they had separated and gotten separate apartments. "I'm glad," Nancy said, "I needed the space away from him. Foster was always on my case about something I didn't do or should have done. I didn't have breakfast with him. I didn't kiss him goodbye. I didn't call during the day. I came home too late. I watched too much TV. I slept on *my* side of the bed. But lately, for some reason, he's back to being sweet and happy with me like he was when I first met him. I guess you were right about our not being able to live together."

Nancy and Foster are perfect examples of the Peter Principle showing up in relationships as well as in corporations. As with the Peter Principle, a relationship is promoted until it reaches the level of its own incompetency and then it is terminated. Most of the time, a breakup results in the couple not even being friends. Rarely are they able to return to the level at which the relationship functioned best. However, Nancy and Foster were both in therapy to dissolve this block to being a couple again, instead of dissolving their relationship. Their imprinted level of incompetency was living together.

Nancy grew up as an only child, alone in the house with her parents most of the time. Her parents were civil to each other, but not friends, and showed very little affection. Her father had a busy career and once Nancy grew old enough to take care of herself, her mother had little to do except shop and play bridge.

"I always thought my mother was childish and spoiled. My Dad worked hard and she didn't seem to understand that. Whenever he came home, she'd nag about his working so late. He'd say he had to because she spent so much money. She was loving to me, but not to him."

Foster's parents shared a similar pattern. "They fought all the time about money." Violent, unhappy, and childish was the way Foster describes them. "My mother was caring, nurturing, and present. My father was always working and griping about bills. I don't remember him there with us at all. Isn't that funny? Cause I know he was. There was this silence all around him. He'd come home and not have anything to say to us. Sometimes he'd be violent with me like he was with Mom."

We could easily see from the Selection Test what the origin of the trouble was between Nancy and Foster. Even though they weren't consciously listening to their parents' interactions when they were little, they had absorbed the pattern. The best way to figure out what happened in both parental relationships was to look at what was showing up between Nancy and Foster now. It is in the period from birth to five years of age that young children accept the environment they are in as "the way it is everywhere" (that is, reality). It is this very unquestioned acceptance of reality that forms the post-hypnotic suggestion for the Inner Couple.

Nancy and Foster were opposites, like their parents, and that complicated their relationship rather than enhancing it. When a problem arises in a set of opposites, each partner has an opposite way of handling the stress. But opposite stress reactions produce an additional crisis and prevent resolution. Couples who are alike will consistently be better able to get through a crisis because they will agree on how to handle it. Under stress they will regress to the same coping patterns.

Psychogenetics made Nancy and Foster aware of their opposite relationship programming on a conscious level. Not that it is that easy to change once the conditioned interactional responses are known, but they were beginning to come out of trance. Instead of focusing on what their partner must change, they were beginning to change themselves. They each would begin to focus on their own negative conditioned reflexes instead of on their partner's.

It was difficult but worthwhile for them to interrupt their own automatic responses and learn to send their partner different cues. The gradual process of getting in control of their own behavior was made easier by role-playing both sets of parents as Nancy and Foster wanted them to be. Maybe it was not too late for these two to save their relationship.

Let's look at a couple who may have waited too long to change.

"It's hard to believe, but how I act with Jim reminds me of my mother! Doing that simple little Selection Test, I realized I acted toward Jim just like my mother was to my father. I didn't like her a lot. She was sneaky, covert, and a manipulator. Still is. Tell me I'm not like that."

We looked at Madeline's Selection Test. She described her mother as a crude, impatient, and loud woman who fussed a lot at everyone.

"Mother said sex wasn't all it was cracked up to be, just a cross a woman has to bear in order to have children. My mother dominated my father. I did that to Jim without even realizing how similar I was to my mother. No wonder he left me."

Jim came in the following week. He stated that Madeline was fine as a wife until the kids came along and then her nerves got to her. "She yelled all the time. I felt sorry for her but didn't want to be home a lot. I just got busier and stayed away more. I don't want to live with her. I've already gotten a job out of town and will only be home once a month. Maybe then I'll be able to stand staying married to her."

His test showed a "rageaholic" father and a peace-maker mother. It was obvious that Jim's mother was his Inner Adult model and his father his Inner Mate Model. Madeline's mother was her Inner Adult and her father was her Inner Mate. This was not good news for her.

"I feel so guilty. Jim is nice like my Daddy was. I was so mean to Jim. Is there anything I can do to make it up to him?"

QUESTIONS:

1. What is it you wanted your Adult Role Model parent to do differently with your Mate Model parent?
2. Can you do that with your mate now?

5. Coming out of Trance

One of the much quoted proverbs in the Neurolinguistic Programming (NLP) community says, "If you always do what you've always done, you'll always get what you've always gotten." It's a statement of cause and effect. It's also a statement about trance. In Psychogenetics, I say, "If you always do what your Inner Couple always did, you'll always get what they've always gotten."

Hundreds of case studies have shown that most people repeat both the selection and the interactional patterns they saw their Adult Role Models follow with each other in childhood. That is not new news. What is new is that most of us don't realize we are in trance, or if we do, we don't depart from the Inner Couple imperative. One of my wisest teachers, Richard Bandler, co-developer of NLP, told me that most people were afraid of hypnosis because they were afraid of going into trance, when indeed what they needed to be afraid of was that they were already in trance. The solution, as I saw in my work with couples, is exactly that—to bring them out of the trance they are living in.

I can stop my friend from standing up in the audience and quacking like a duck if I tell her what she has been hypnotized to do *before* she starts to quack. I can interrupt her trance reaction before the stimulus presents itself, but not after or during. The post-hypnotic suggestion will take over immediately upon her hearing the word *duck*, but its power can be greatly weakened if her conscious mind is aware of what is coming rather than being caught by surprise and thrown into an automatic reaction.

"The difference between transition and crisis is preparation," Gail Sheehy said years ago in her groundbreaking bestseller *Passages*. Being prepared ahead of time is vital in order to break the trance. The conscious mind must be prepared to recognize and interrupt the previous induction before the subconscious mind hears the command and automatically takes over the controls.

It is important that the conscious mind become familiar with responses other than the old stress reactions from the Inner Adult in childhood. That's why all the three-chair exercises I've developed are roleplayed in the first person present tense, as if you are watching your parents in your childhood. You practice them in order to reprogram your subconscious with a new and better response pattern than the ones your Adult Role Model showed you. Roleplaying unlocks even more of your hidden memories and uncovers who your parents really were, how they interacted with each other, which parent you identified with, and which parent's traits you are exhibiting or disowning.

I quote from Robert Anton Wilson in his book *Quantum Psychology:*

> Where [Timothy] Leary and [Stanislaus] Grof, like Jung and Freud, assumed the non-ego information, not known to the brain, must come from the genes, Dr. Rupert Sheldrake, a biologist and author of *A New Science of Life,* knew that genes cannot carry such information. He therefore posited a non-local field, like those in quantum theory, which he named the morphogenetic field. This field communicates *between* genes but cannot be found *in* the genes—just as Johnny Carson "travels" between TV sets but cannot be found *in* any of the TV sets that receive him.

People are amazed and dismayed when they discover how many traits of the Inner Adult parent they are acting out in their own adult relationships. Like a matched set, the traits of the Mate Model parent usually show up in the choice of a partner. Most of the personality and behavior traits of the parent you did not identify with are now your subconscious requisites for a mate. Your Inner Couple is a projection of your home video from childhood days. What is still showing on the TV screen in your mind's eye is the relationship your parents had when you were an infant, a toddler, and a young child.

It's time for a remake.

The Cycle of Abuse as it repeats in the Inner Couple

If you come from a set of parents where one adult was abusive to the other, as an adult you are programmed under stress to:

A) Abuse your partner
B) Be abused by your partner
C) Be self-abusive, or
D) Have a self-abusive partner

—Anne Teachworth

6. Abused or Abandoned? Pick One

"David is nice and everything, but he's not my type at all," Rita protested to me. "But considering what's happened over the last few years with my type, that probably is the best news I've had in years."

Rita had recently been introduced to her best friend's cousin from another city and for the first time was considering trying an out-of-town relationship with someone not her type. Rita's Selection Test showed this guy was indeed the opposite of her usual partners. He was more like Rita's father. Rita's usual type, of course, wasn't "nice and everything," to use her analysis. Rita's usual partner was selfish.

A lawyer with a prestigious firm, Rita consistently picked the misunderstood loner type. "Leo needed me," she had said about her most recent disastrous relationship, "and you know I always like to be needed. Even though Leo aggravated me with his demands, I couldn't leave him. He finally left me." Rita's previous three relationships had ended the same way, with those men leaving her. "After all I did for them, too," she wailed.

Rita had come to me to change her selection pattern. "I'm tired of being a nice person and getting trampled on," she proclaimed on her first visit to my office. After only two sessions, she was already realizing how her initial attraction to a certain personality type bore an amazing resemblance to her father's choice of her mother for his mate.

"My previous therapist kept telling me I had unfinished business with my father—that if I'd work on it I wouldn't pick mates who mistreated or left me. But I knew I wasn't picking mates like him—I was actually like him. My mates were like my demanding mother, and I was getting abused by them just like my father was by her. My mother was always complaining nobody understood her. That everyone was against her and that my devoted father really didn't care about her. Nothing he did could change her mind."

If Rita decided to experiment with dating David, someone not her type, the problem she would have in a relationship with him was predictable. Rita herself would switch Inner Couple roles without consciously wanting to, and this time her mother's whiny, demanding behaviors would be likely to surface in her instead of in her partner. Much to her dismay, Rita would find that her behaviors with David resembled her mother's miserable behavior with her father, and as a result, for the first time, Rita would not like herself as much as she liked her mate. Her self-esteem would suffer.

The Selection Test allowed Rita to understand what was happening with her. Consistently she had picked her mother's type in order to avoid becoming that type herself. Rita had subconsciously picked lovers who filled her mother's Inner Mate role, which kept Rita abused by her mate, just as her father had been by his.

"If I'm anything with David like my mother was with my father, I'll shoot myself," Rita told me when I informed her of her impending temporary role model shift. However, I wanted her to purposefully practice her mother's behaviors in this relationship with David, should she choose to accept the challenge.

"You're telling me in order to break the trance, I'll have to be like Mom was and understand her from the inside? But I don't have to stay that way, do I? Maybe David will really shoot me. He'll have every right. My mother was terrible. I'm going to have to fix her if I have to be her. I can't stand being her the way she was."

It was actually easier for Rita to fix her mother's abusive tendencies while she was in her role in the relationship, than to try to fix these same traits in her partner. That's what Rita had tried to do in her previous relationships.

Unlike Lori in a previous chapter, Rita was now willing to experience her mother as her Adult Role Model and change her instead of picking partner after partner like her mother and trying to change them. By switching role models consciously, Rita would actually free herself from the imbedded post-hypnotic suggestion. Previously, Rita had to select only partners who were like Mom so she herself could be like her favorite parent. Rita had been doing what her father did when he got married. He picked an unhappy partner and then tried to make his partner happy. Co-dependency is the name of that game. Rita, like her father, had been trying to love her partner enough to make him feel understood. She was trying to do all the very same things that her father spent his entire married life trying to achieve with her mother, and never did.

David, on the other hand, was the perfect mate for Rita's role model shift, because he was unlike Rita's other choices. Rita's choice of David showed me that some change in Rita's attraction pattern had already occurred because David's Inner Couple was not the same as Rita's. David's parents were not opposites. They were very happy and had a lot in common. It would be easy for David to fill Rita's loving father's position, the Inner Adult role that Rita had played in her previous relationships, simply because David's parents were alike and *not* abusing a mate truly did come easy for him.

For the first time, Rita experienced her mother's position in her interactions with David, and had an opportunity to investigate what it was like for her mother to be in an adult-adult relationship with her possessive father. Some of her father's negative traits that Rita had been unaware of in herself when he was her Inner Adult, did, of course, show up in David and begin to aggravate Rita as she assumed her mother's position for a change. Some of Rita's mother's traits that Rita had hated became positive to Rita as she grew to understand her mother's reactions from the inside of her mother's role. Uncovering the positive characteristics in her disliked mother's personality and the negative characteristics in her much loved father's, neutralized the post-hypnotic suggestion and broke her parents' subconscious hold on Rita's future relationship pattern.

EXERCISE:

Write five negative traits of your favorite parent and five positive traits of your other parent to change your perspective. See your parents as the adult people they were to each other, not as the parents they were to you.

7. Lady-in-Waiting

Let's go back over each of Heather's relationships since her divorce seven years ago. There were seven of them, three married lovers and four unmarried. Checking the last three married men she was involved with, Heather realized they were all dominant, like her mother's boyfriends. Two of the men Heather had affairs with stayed married. Both broke up with Heather. The third man with whom Heather was sexually involved, Austin, left his wife for Heather, but within three months Heather broke up with him.

"Things weren't working out well," she said. "Austin changed from an interesting guy to a super needy guy. He wanted to see me all the time. I felt crowded. I couldn't stand being around him anymore. Why?"

As an unmarried, available male, Austin no longer fit Heather's Inner Couple pattern. Getting her mate to put her first had always been the unattainable challenge that Heather, with her mistress mother as her Inner Adult Role Model, had taken on and never accomplished. Born to an unmarried mother and her married lover, Heather had no precedent in her history of her Inner Adult Role Model mother ever getting what she wanted from her mate. She could only long for it.

Programmed only for the mistress role, when someone wanted to marry her, Heather had to end the relationship. Her mother had always put her partner first and he had always put her last. It was the Inner Couple imperative that Heather saw them act out daily. Heather's father left her mother. Therefore, Heather's inherited pattern was that she, as her Adult Role Model father, left the one who loved her and that Inner Mate cried.

I asked Heather about the unmarried men with whom she has been in relationships. I knew the answer before she told me, but we went over each of them just as we had with the married ones. The pattern became apparent. In all cases, the available unmarried men were more like her available mother in personality and behavior. But once Heather had sex, she left them just as her father had left his mistresses, one of whom was Heather's mother.

"That's an amazing insight. Now I know why this happened over and over to me in relationships. I never thought I was in a trance. It never even occurred to me before this moment," she exclaimed. "How do I stop wasting my time like this? I don't want my relationships to be anything like my father's *or* my mother's with any of their mates."

We started by having Heather become her mother and consciously reprogram her responses to her mate. Next, she did the same by becoming her father and, through roleplay, practicing being available and caring to Heather's mother.

"I needed to have other loving role models, too. Life would have been so much easier if I'd had two positive examples. Let's imagine my mother finding a good unmarried man for a change and then staying with him," Heather suggested as she saw the new Psychogenetic possibilities presented to her. "You know, my ineffective patterns are so obvious to me now that I'm looking at myself from this perspective. Before, I didn't stop to think about where I was heading until the relationship was over. That seems really stupid now. I let passion make a lot of decisions for me and then when the passion was fading, I exited stage left just like you know who."

8. *Alternate Role Models*

If your current or past partners are not similar to either of your biological parents, check to see how similar they are to other adults who stayed in your home when you were a child—that is, a parent's mate, step-parent, grandparent, aunt, uncle, older sister and her husband, older brother and his wife, babysitter, or nanny.

The adults who were present in your live-in environment in your earliest years have had the most significant impact on your subconscious mind and may have become your alternate Inner Mate and Inner Adult Models, in addition to your own parents.

Adults who were present in your life after ten years of age have had a less significant impact, but may still have become your alternate role models.

You may use this chart to describe your family of origin when you were ten to sixteen years of age—during the teenage imprint years, which have a lessened but still important impact on you.

EXERCISE:

1. Fill in the alternate Selection Chart on the next page if there were any other adults living in the house with you for any length of time when you were sixteen years of age or less. Describe each person as the adult he or she was then and also describe your parent's couple relationship with that person then.

2. Describe your relationship then with each live-in person. At what ages in your childhood was this person part of an alternate Inner Couple model for you?

3. Place a plus (+) or minus (–) by each person's name to describe your early experience and relationship with each one you list.

4. Put a check mark by your favorite adult in that Inner Couple, which may have changed since early childhood.

5. On the Alternate Family History page, which follows the chart, describe how you experienced this family during your childhood from birth to ten, and/or during your teenage years, especially if there was a change, that is, death of a parent, divorce, abandonment, etc.

2. Describe the female parent (or stepmother, father's live-in girlfriend, aunt, grandmother, nanny, maid, etc.) as the adult she was when you were a child or teenager:

Alternate

Step One: Childhood

8. Describe these two adults' relationship with each other when you were a child or teenager:

6. Female Parent-Child/Teenager Relationship:

4. Describe how this female was as a parent when you were a child or teenager:

1. Describe yourself as the child you were (0-10 years of age) or as the teenager up to 16 years old:

Selection Test™
History Chart

3. Describe the male parent (or stepfather, mother's live-in boyfriend, aunt, grandfather, etc.) as the adult he was when you were a child or teenager:

7. Male Parent-Child/Teenager Relationship:

5. Describe how this male was as a parent when you were a child or teenager:

ALTERNATE FAMILY HISTORY EXERCISE

VII. THE HOMEWORK

A problem cannot be solved by the same thinking which created it.

—Albert Einstein

1. The Shadow Side

The most important factor in reprogramming the Inner Couple is to experience what it was like for your Inner Mate Model to be with his or her Inner Adult model, as you will see with our next two couples. In each example, the partners had to roleplay both sets of parents several times in order to change their Inner Couple programming.

Example #1: For Terri, a forty-year-old woman, roleplaying her disliked Inner Mate Model/father was a major personality shift. Last week I assigned Terri some homework, which she didn't do. The exercise for Terri was to imagine whom she would have chosen for a wife if she had been her father at twenty-one. Her father was not her favorite parent. Her Inner Adult/mother was.

"All of a sudden it came to me. It's not the thought of being my father, it's the thought of being married to a mate who ignored me like my mother ignored him that's kept me from getting into any permanent relationship. My mother was so good to us kids, but just awful to him now that I stop to think about it. I can see that all too clearly now. I've only had two options. Be like her or be like him. My mother had a real cold side to her. But I'd much rather be withdrawn like her than be ignored like he was."

Milton, Terri's Inner Mate boy friend, was in a similar Inner Couple trance. Listen to his avoidance level:

"Terri's mother and mine are alike. Terri's exactly like my mother, so she's my Inner Mate, right? My father and Terri's father are also alike. But in no way am I like my father! It's impossible." Milton, of course, is blind to seeing who is his own Inner Adult Role Model.

Like most people, Milton could see his partner more clearly than he could see himself. The part of Milton's personality that he was not willing to recognize was his Inner Adult/father, who was showing up unannounced in Milton's relationship with Terri. Terri, of course, could easily see how Milton's personality traits and behavior resembled his father's.

For homework, I asked Milton to turn back to his Selection Test, look at how he had described his father as an adult person with his mother, and find an instance in his own life when he, Milton, exhibited each one of his father's traits with Terri.

"That's not fair," he said to me, already realizing the outcome. "You tricked me. You saw what I'd written down for him, didn't you?"

Most definitely!

Example #2: Now let's explore Jill's resistance to her Shadow Side—the complimentary opposite model in her subconscious that guided her in picking a mate. Back for her third session, Jill hadn't yet done the homework I had assigned her in the first session, which was to write a history of her mother and father's relationship during her early childhood.

"My mother thinks she is perfect and everyone else is at fault. She doesn't think there is anything wrong with her ever. I'm tired of talking to her in therapy sessions and out," Jill said, explaining why she hadn't done her homework.

But that which we resist, persists. I told Jill I wanted her to roleplay her mother and father talking to each other, not her Inner Child/self talking to her mother. I certainly did not intend to focus again on Jill's relationship with either of her parents. Her parents' Inner Couple relationship was the negative interactional imprint that had been consistently overlooked in Jill's previous therapy. It was this Inner Couple pattern that set the precedent for the problematic repetition that Jill exhibited in her own marriage.

"What good would talking to my parents do now?" Jill inquired as we sat and talked about her own relationship history. But non-communication, withholding feelings, and long silences were also the order of the day with Jill's husband and child. Comparing these relationships with Jill's Selection Test, I was not surprised to see that the emotional distance Jill showed to them was an inherited interactional pattern handed down from her Inner Adult Role Model. But Jill didn't recognize it.

"I can see how my husband is a lot like my father, but in no way am I like my mother. I'm not anywhere near that messed up," Jill insisted.

Well, that was highly improbable! Jill, like the rest of us, was a lot like both of her parents but particularly like one of them. In this case, it was most apparent (as in *a-parent*) by Jill's denials of her own behavior that she was indeed like her mother in a relationship.

Like Jill, most clients can easily recognize which parent their partner is most like. However, they are usually unable or unwilling to own up to their Inner Adult if that role model is not their favorite parent. What is most enlightening about the Selection Test is that the descriptions of your Inner Adult from the conditioning period (birth to ten years old) identify your post-hypnotic suggestions. Roleplaying provides an opportunity to know what your Inner Adult Role Model parent was feeling back then by experiencing his or her imprinted feelings inside you. They were then like yours are now.

THE PSYCHOGENETICS™ SYSTEM
CHILDHOOD HISTORY CHART REFERENCE GUIDE

Inner Child (#1): The subconscious part of your personality that retains all the memories and feelings you had as a child. Your description of yourself as a child indicates your adult level of *self-esteem* and predicts how you will react under stress.

Inner Adult (#2 or #3): The kind of partner you were programmed to be in your own couple relationship. The parent whom you are most like as an adult was your *Adult Role Model* and predicts your *fate*. Your description of this person reveals the latent adult personality that has been hiding inside you from childhood and your *self-image* as an adult.

Inner Mate (#2 or #3): The kind of partner you were programmed to select for your own couple relationship. The parent your mate is most like was your *Mate Model* and predicts your *type*. You are attracted to and search for a partner with these traits, based on the post-hypnotic suggestion from childhood to find a mate like the your Adult Role Model parent found.

Inner Parent (#4 or #5): The kind of parent you were programmed to be by your Adult Role Model's parenting example. If your female parent on the chart (#2) is identified as your Adult Role Model, then #4 is your Inner Parent and #6 (your mother-child relationship) is your Self-Talk. However, if your male parent on the chart (#3) is identified as your Adult Role Model, then #5 is your Inner Parent and #7 (your father-child relationship) is your Self-Talk.

Self-Talk (#6 or #7): The way you talk to yourself internally, the way you feel about what you feel, and particularly what you say to yourself under stress. The way you described your relationship as a child with your Inner Adult/Inner Parent is now how you talk to yourself internally.

Inner Couple (#8): Your subconscious model for an adult relationship. Your description of your parents' early adult-adult interaction reveals how your own adult-adult relationships are programmed to be from selection to solution. Recreating your parents' relationship is your subconscious goal in adulthood, regardless of which adult role you are in at the time.

2. Letting Go Is Hard to Do

"I left my homework at the office. I had a hard time doing it and then I couldn't remember where I put it. I guess I must have some resistance to changing my internal couple programming, right?" Dottie said as she came in twenty minutes late for her fourth session.

Yep! That's one of the reasons I give clients home-work—to find out just how much resistance they have to letting go of their old ineffective pattern. Lack of any other programmed solutions to their relationship causes people to hold on to their parents' options for security. It helps them to know what to do under stress.

We were in the process of redesigning Dottie's couple relationship patterns, which were modeled after her parents' negative interactions. Dottie, like her Inner Adult/mother, had been unhappy with her husband since she married him and had been trying to get him to change instead of working on herself. That's a popular, non-effective method. I told her a better one.

The only way I've found to change your partner is to change yourself, and the best way to change yourself is to first change your memory of your Adult precedent under stress. Then, with an improved Inner Adult in her, Dottie would send differ-ent cues and her partner would have to change his response to her. I was sure she didn't want to hear that.

"As a child, I wanted my mother to stay with my father, and after she left, I wanted her to go back to him. Every night, I would pray she wouldn't leave my father. Now, as an adult, I find that I can't stay in a relation-ship anymore unless everything goes smoothly. At the first sign of trouble, I want to get out, too. I guess I'm thinking about doing what she did," Dottie surmised. "Right?"

After three years of marriage, she could indeed be

right and wrong at the same time. I told Dottie that her impatience with things not being perfect was most likely the exact same reason her mother left her father in the first place. Dottie's marriage was the one in trouble now. I didn't want Dottie to follow in her mother's footsteps. I wanted Dottie to change her mother's pattern and learn to stay and solve her relationship problems with her husband instead of giving up and leaving.

"My friends tell me I have a fear of commitment," she said. "You bet I do! My father was committed to my mother and she left him anyhow. Then she moved in with this 'rageaholic' and wouldn't leave him."

We set up three chairs—one for her mother, one for her father, and one for Dottie as a child watching them. One at a time we reviewed the stages of her mother's two relationships. We started by creating a false positive memory—saving her mother's marriage to Dottie's father.

Roleplaying her mother, who was her Inner Adult Role Model, Dottie said to her father, "Hank, I've decided not to leave you for Howard. I think we should get counseling so we can learn to work out our problems. I love you. I want to stay."

Next we had Dottie, as her mother, talk to her mother's boyfriend.

"Howard, I've decided to go back to my husband and work out my relationship with him. I realized in counseling that the problems I have with him can be fixed and for the sake of my child, I think I shouldn't divorce."

Then I had Dottie as her father tell her mother that he not only forgives her for walking out on him, but is willing to take her back, providing they seek counseling. Dottie, moving to the child chair, smiled when she heard her father say those words.

"That's what I really wanted to hear him say, that he would take Mommy back after she went to live with

Howard. That makes me so happy. Mommy was too proud to ever ask Daddy to forgive her. She stayed with that horrible boyfriend of hers rather than admit to my father she'd made a mistake. She couldn't even imagine he would forgive her. But I will imagine he did."

Dottie moved to the Mother chair and said out loud, "Hank, I made a mistake and I'm not too proud to admit it. I shouldn't have left you. I want to come back if you can forgive me."

What we were doing here was creating an alternate reality for Dottie to remember and repeat in her own relationship so she could stay in her marriage.

3. Forgiveness Exercise

The following is an effective exercise you can use if you are having trouble letting go of a past hurt in your relationship. The act of first identifying and then imagining getting exactly what you want from your partner creates a receptivity inside you where forgiveness can actually happen. The creating of a reunion in the future also produces an eagerness to let go of the past and make room for something new to occur in your relationship. Repeated practice creates a truly self-fulfilling prophecy instead of a non-fulfilling one.

1. What could your partner do in the future for you to forgive him/her?
2. Write a story about him/her doing it.
3. Read the story out loud.
4. Set up three empty chairs, one for you, one for your partner now and one for him/her in the future.
5. Sit in your chair and look at the your partner sitting in the "now" chair. Watch him/her get up and move over to the future chair. Look at his or her face and see him/her say the words that you want to hear.
6. Roleplay him/her actually doing it.
7. Respond as you would if your partner had actually said it.
8. Feel how you would feel if your partner had said it.
9. Move to your partner's chair and feel how your partner would feel if he or she had just said it, and hear your own response.
10. Now tell this story out loud three times, in the past tense as if you are already in the future and this forgiveness and reunion had already happened.

NOTE: This exercise also works well if you need to forgive yourself for something you did.

4. Changing Memories

Retelling exercises have been particularly helpful for many clients. Make sure you rewrite the story of your family the way you want it to be. Make sure it has a happy ending. Keith liked the idea so much he started two generations back, changing his family memories and writing a new history of his grandmother and grandfather, too. For the first time, he imagined how things would have been if his grandmother had been able to show affection to her husband and son, Keith's father.

"My grandfather might never have had that affair, and my father might never have grown up cold and unloving like his mother. I could even carry this new scenario a little further. My father wouldn't have picked a wife like my mother, who didn't get any warmth or affection from him. She ended up getting involved with someone else like my father's father had. Can you follow that? It would have changed everything that came afterwards if my grandmother had only been loving."

Next Keith wrote a new memory of his mother and father and read it out loud before we roleplayed it.

"Usually, and for no reason other than sheer meanness, my father would rage at my mother. She would just sit silently and cry," started the new memory. "One day when I was eight, a funny thing happened. My mother finally stood up for herself and told Dad off. 'You have no right to criticize me like that,' my mother continued. 'I've had enough. Stop it or get out of here.' My father's jaw fell open. I didn't think he knew what was happening. After the longest silence I'd ever heard from him, he apologized, and then he said the two words I never thought I would ever hear him say to anyone in his whole life . . . 'You're right.' It was a great day in the history of the Hines family."

After he roleplayed his imagined story, I had Keith retell it out loud to transfer it from his right brain's imagination to his left brain's memory.

"I like having those new memories of my grandfather and my mother. It makes me smile to remember my grandmother and father giving their mates compliments for a change instead of criticisms. It's as if that really happened. I sure wish it had. I'm going to pretend it did. It makes me feel good just considering it could have. I never stopped to think that my affair with Gail was programmed into me by both my mother's and grandfather's example. I always wondered why I fooled around when I knew good and well it could cost me my marriage. Will the homework have any effect on my relationship with my wife, Suzanne?" Keith asked. "Unfortunately, I've already had the affair and my marriage is in big trouble."

In the next therapy session, I had Suzanne rewrite her parents' history. Her parental set closely matched Keith's. Her cruel, angry mother was her Inner Adult model and her lonely, sad father was her Inner Mate Model. It was her father whom Keith represented in her Inner Couple. She was like her mother. In Suzanne's new script, her mother started an argument with her father, but instead of leaving as he usually did, Suzanne's father snapped back at her mother.

"This is it. It's over. I've had enough of your rage. Get out and don't come back until you can be a loving wife and mother."

Suzanne described how she went to school that morning and when she came back, her Inner Adult mother was crying.

"When I walked in the door, I overheard her telling my father how much she loved him and how she didn't want to make him unhappy. He said he'd give her one last chance. From then on, she stopped fussing about everything and started smiling and being affectionate.

It's hard to believe, knowing my mother, but it's harder on me not believing it. Remembering this story gives me comfort and direction on how to be with Keith and my children from now on. I don't want him to leave me for that other woman. I want him to stay. That's my happy ending to this story. I know it's not true, but it's better than the Inner Couple script I've had all my life."

EXERCISE:

1. Look back at your grandparents' relationships and realize the impact those two Inner Couples had on your parents. What do you know about their couple relationships and how were they similar to your parents' couple relationship and yours?
2. Rewrite both sets of grandparents' relationships so your parents can grow up with loving role models in positive environments.
3. How would your parents each have been different then?

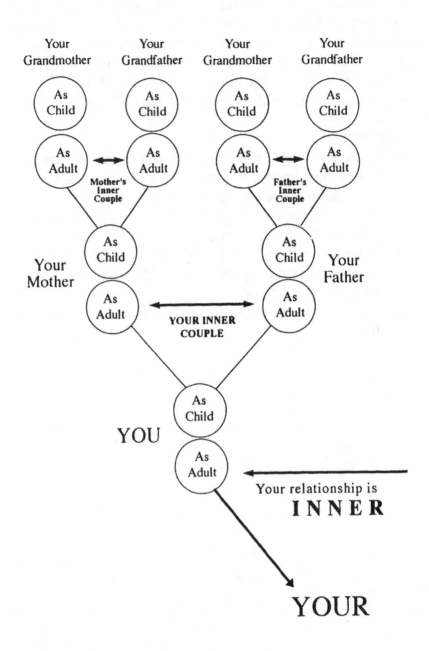

Your Grandmother — As Child — As Adult

Your Grandfather — As Child — As Adult

Your Grandmother — As Child — As Adult

Your Grandfather — As Child — As Adult

Mother's Inner Couple

Father's Inner Couple

Your Mother — As Child — As Adult

Your Father — As Child — As Adult

YOUR INNER COUPLE

YOU — As Child — As Adult

Your relationship is
I N N E R

YOUR

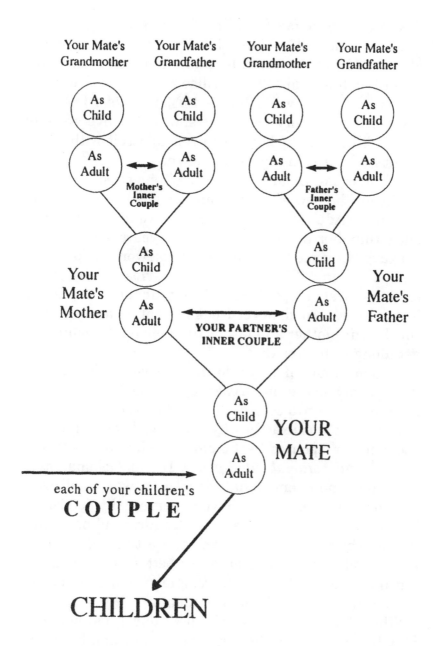

5. Creating False Positive Memories

Alison came in sobbing. I knew her family history already. Alison's mother had had a nervous breakdown when her husband left her. Alison was only five years old then. Now it was Alison's husband Zeke who had walked out. Twenty-four now, she had a five-year-old son. I did not want history to repeat itself with her. I spent an hour calming Alison down.

"It's just like Daddy did to Mom," she cried.

Alison's homework had been designed to reprogram her Inner Adult/mother so that she could react differently than her mother had all those years ago.

I gave her some Psychogenetic homework to do for the next session. "Write three scenarios where your mother—first, stops freaking out about your father leaving her; second, never freaks out at all about it; and third, your mother and father fix their relationship and get along well after that."

"I don't know if I can do that," Alison said. "I can't imagine my mother not freaking out and definitely can't imagine those two ever fixing their marriage."

Well, that was exactly why I asked Alison to imagine those new responses to the old stimulus. In his recent bestseller *Emotional Intelligence,* Daniel Goleman says ". . . the genetic emotional disposition we are all born with does not necessarily have to perpetually determine how we respond emotionally to our surroundings." This is why children who are given more training in emotional and social competence are better at not regressing into the familiar stress reactions that are demonstrated in their family environments.

When Alison came back the next day, I had her role-play her mother and father, once as they had been and then three times as she wanted them to be. She reenacted their divorce while roleplaying her mother relating to her father in whatever non-freakout ways Alison had been able to imagine. We were imbedding three new Inner Adult reactions into Alison's subconscious, thereby creating alternative behavioral precedents for her in this stress situation.

These exercises did, in fact, install three false positive memories in Alison's Inner Adult/mother, so that Alison now would have some positive coping choices in her reactions to problematic life situations. She would be able to remember her mother not freaking out, and coping well with stress. This altered her Inner Adult's behavior both in her past and her present.

When people do not change their parents' post-hypnotic suggestions, the subconscious mind does not have any alternative options under stress, and in an unfamiliar situation, it automatically regresses to what has been imprinted. Even though the conscious mind may want to behave differently, it can not create a positive reaction under stress. It's hard enough to think how to change one's own behavior when we are not in stress. In the midst of turmoil, it becomes even harder to think rationally. Even counting to ten is extremely difficult at those times. Under stress, your parents' Inner Couple behavior immediately shows on the screen in your mind's eye. We must therefore implant a new response and put a new parental precedent on that screen. What goes into our subconscious from birth to ten years old determines what comes out later in our Inner Adult behavior, unless we change it ourselves.

As Caroline Myss says in *Anatomy of the Spirit,* "Creative energy breaks us out of habitual patterns of behavior, thoughts, and relationships." That certainly was true here. Simply reimagining positive scenarios changed Alison's stress reaction completely.

By the next session, she had calmed down dramatically and already decided to go ahead with the divorce.

"You know," she said "I never loved Zeke anyhow. I

only married him because I was pregnant. We got off to a bad start. That was true for my parents, too. My mother was pregnant when she got married. I think the problem was in my selection of Zeke for a husband to start with, not in his leaving me. Neither of us was happy with each other. We just couldn't admit it before."

6. Opposites Attract, Then Detract

Natalie was a young ad agency executive. Extremely respected in her field, she had, however, not enjoyed the same level of success in her personal life.

"I always end up hurting the guys who are my best friends, the ones who are the nicest to me, because they want to date me and I'm not attracted to them. Worse yet, I get hurt by the ones whom I am attracted to. I've always gone after guys that I don't have anything in common with.

"It's been that way since the seventh grade, actually. I was always attracted to the boys who teased me. I remember the first time how crushed I was when I found out Bobby told my best friend he liked her more than me. Then he left her the exact same way. The boys who wanted me to be their girlfriend weren't attractive to me. I've always fallen in love with the jerks. The kind that have a new girl every week. I never told any of them how much they hurt me. But they did. Now I'm hurting men the same way they hurt me. I'm doing the same thing with Gary, my best friend, even though I don't want to. We have such fun together, love to do the same things, and we laugh all the time, but when he starts wanting more, I move away.

"My mother always told me opposites attract, that being with someone like myself would be boring and that somebody different from me would make my life interesting. Now I realize being with someone like me isn't boring unless I'm boring. As successful as I am on the job, I don't know what to talk about when I'm alone with a guy and it's not business. We usually just sit around, smoke, and end up making out."

I told Natalie that was what would happen as long as she picked guys she had nothing in common with but sex. She'd get bored and not have anything to talk about.

Natalie's mother and father were not communicative people either, and Natalie described them as rarely talking about feelings. In fact, she said, they didn't have much in common.

"They started off in crisis and have been there ever since. I know they had to get married cause my mother got pregnant with me. I hate the idea of me being the reason they had to stay together. I also hate the idea that I got married because I got pregnant, too. I guess my husband loved me, but I didn't love him. I wasn't attracted to him anymore. My father had affairs for years, but my mother never said anything to him about them. I don't think she really cared one way or the other what he did or who he did it with. I didn't stick around my husband long enough for him to have affairs on me, or me on him. I got bored being married to him."

Homework for Natalie was to reprogram her early relationship patterning. Notice that her repetitious pair bonds always had one partner who cared and one who didn't. Opposites each time. Never alike. Natalie's first assignment was to rewrite her experience with her seventh-grade boyfriend. I asked her to pretend she had told Bobby how hurt she was, in order to get her to release the withheld emotion that she had been carrying around inside her. Then I had Natalie roleplay saying it to Bobby.

Next, I asked Natalie to roleplay her mother giving her a different message about relationships.

"You will be happier if you are with someone who is like you," she imagined her mother telling her at seven years old. Happily, Natalie imagined her mother getting dressed to go to a party with Natalie's father. Then her mother told her how much she and her father enjoyed the same things in life.

Natalie liked to remember her mother saying how important it was for a couple to have similar interests and values, that it made life interesting.

"I know Mama didn't really say that, but I love imagining she did. My mother was always so bored with my father. It's nice to remember at least one time when she was excited by him. Even if I have to make it up, I feel better than not having any fun memories of them together at all," she said.

In her next exercise, Natalie pretended Gary was in one of the chairs and told him that she was not attracted to him, but that she loved him and he was her best friend. Following my lead, she told Gary that she wanted his help in changing her Inner Couple pattern. She now realized that unless she changed it, she would get herself involved with another lover with whom she had nothing in common. Natalie told me she was afraid to tell Gary those intimate feelings in real life.

"He might take it seriously," she said, "Then what will I do?"

I was expecting Natalie to tell me she didn't want Gary to fall in love with her because she might end up leaving him, but instead she said she was afraid she'd fall in love with him and he would leave her—just as her father had finally left her mother. The abandonment program was deeply imbedded.

I asked her to rewrite her Mother and Dad's history so that she overheard her father telling her mother he had changed his pattern and wanted to be attentive and faithful to her. He would ask her to join him on some of his out-of-town trips to interesting places.

In the next session, we roleplayed that scene with Natalie sitting in for both parents. She loved it. Then I asked Natalie to be her Inner Child/self and tell us her memory of a time when her mother and father were both affectionate with each other, and from then on whenever he left to go someplace, he took his wife with him for company. This added step of retelling the imagined story was necessary to transfer Natalie's right brain wish to the left side of her brain, where memory resides. The transfer creates a positive precedent—a new Inner Couple option—and creates a space inside Natalie for something different to happen with her own relationships.

Next, I had Natalie again retell the incident from memory, only this time as if it had happened five years later in her childhood. She remembered her parents still in that loving space with each other. Indeed, my very suggestion created a domino effect in her Inner Couple patterning. The memory of her imagined memory brought her Inner Adult/mother forward into time and imprinted five years of happiness in Natalie's Inner Couple programming. The imprint interrupted Natalie's subconscious search for an opposite Inner Mate and brought her out of her Inner Adult trance.

"Do all opposites have relationship problems?" she asked me.

"No," I replied, "only if their parents did."

However, most couples who are opposites will certainly have more conflict than couples who are alike. Couples who are alike usually come from parents who were also alike and agreed on most things. Their relationships are usually a lot more conflict free. The child of a couple who are alike in most ways will be programmed to think that's the way married couples are supposed to be with each other.

The fact is that couples who have parents who are alike rarely show up in couple therapy, nor do couples who have two "plus" parents with a "plus" relationship. However, like Natalie, many people did not have parents who were alike or "pluses" and therefore didn't have models for wonderful relationships passed on to them. When they ask me, "What can be done about us?" I say, as I did with Natalie, "Let's first see what can be done about your parents."

Natalie continued her Psychogenetic sessions for

another month. She and Gary went to Europe together, and when she came back for her next session, she walked in laughing.

"Gary and I had such a great time together on the trip, I've moved into his place. I figured out what the problem was with us before. We were too much alike. You know how I've always been attracted to opposites, not that I could get along with them either. I had plenty friends who were like me, but my lovers weren't. Now I want to be with someone I like. A friend I love will work out better in the long run than someone I'm just attracted to. I know well how bad those turn out for me. Do you think I'm cured?"

She was certainly out of her trance and ready to lead a different kind of life than her mother and father had.

7. *Like Mother, like Son*

Casey's first wife was demanding, angry, and always gone, like his father. Although Casey worked long, hard hours trying to please and provide for his wife, she was never happy with him or the fruits of his labor.

"I'm still trying to make her happy and we've been divorced two years. Nothing I do is enough. I loved her so much but she didn't ever love me."

Casey was slowly coming out of his trance and was finally involved with someone who was very loving to him.

"Unlike my typical choice of a female, Cathy seems to want to spend a lot of time with me, cook for me, and she's easy to get along with, too," he boasted.

Not Casey's usual type of girlfriend. Casey's parents were opposites. His stern father, a successful, demanding, angry man, was a workaholic who had had numerous affairs. He had always been out somewhere. The mother, sweet, compliant, and quiet, had always stayed at home. After about fifteen years of marriage, Casey's mother walked out on his father, never to return. Long used, misused, and abused, she went on to start a successful career and married again, this time choosing a man who waited on her hand and foot.

In effect, Casey's mother took on the Inner Couple role her husband had played in their first marriage and picked for her second husband someone who treated her like she had treated her first husband. Vowing to never love anyone that much again, she switched Inner Couple roles and became the dominant, workaholic partner and left the subservient role for her second husband. This was what Casey was doing now.

It was interesting to hear Casey talk about how his new girlfriend wanted a commitment from him.

"Cathy loves me so much, but I just don't have that

special feeling about her. I feel guilty because she does so much for me all the time, and never complains. Heck, she does it before I even have to ask her. But I'm just not in love with her. I don't know what's missing."

Well, what was missing was abuse. Simply put, Casey was programmed to be in a relationship where one partner uses, misuses, or abuses the other, and unless the partner he picked did that to him, he would not feel subconsciously connected to her. The relationship pattern would not be familiar. The only programmed choice Casey had to fulfill his family's Inner Couple imperative was to use, misuse, or abuse Cathy. That is what Casey was about to do to Cathy, even though he didn't understand why.

"I know I used to pick women who took advantage of me. But what are you saying? That I want to leave Cathy because she is too good to me or I'll have to abuse her in order to stay? That's weird, but I actually have tried to get her mad at me a few times. I don't thank her or treat her nice. She even told me the other day that I take advantage of her and take her for granted. But I don't think I could abuse her. She loves me too much."

I explained the Cycle of Abuse. **If a child comes from an abusive Inner Couple, that child, as an adult, will either pick an abusive partner, be the abusive partner, be involved with a self-abusive partner, or become self-abusive while in a couple relationship.** Since Casey's Adult Role Model parent had been abused by her mate in Casey's childhood, and Cathy was not abusing him, Casey was subconsciously compelled to be like his abusive father. Casey's mother had also switched roles in her second marriage. So Casey's idea of a relationship still contained one abuser and one abused. Under stress he would regress to this familiar Inner Couple model unless we implanted a memory of both his parents as nurturing, loving, and supporting of each other.

The homework assignment for Casey was to write five scenes where his mother and father were good to each other. Then we roleplayed each scene during the next session. The fact that Casey readily imagined these possibilities demonstrated his willingness to let go of both his mother's and father's negative role modeling.

Changing his Inner Couple in his mind's eye was the only effective way to change his subconscious patterning now. Each time Casey reenacted a caring scene from his parents' past, he was reprogramming his own future with his mate.

8. Like Mother, like Daughter

Kate was very quiet, like her mother. Married to a very aggressive business man much older than she, at thirty-five she now had two children, a boy and a girl.

"Dad was very much the boss. My father was a very successful business man who ran roughshod over my mother. She was real mousy around him."

Kate had one brother, who, as she described him, was the boss in his family, too. Kate's mother and father divorced after fifteen years. Her father had remarried but her mother never did. "Being married to your father cured me of ever wanting to live with a man again," Kate's mother Gretchen had told her after the divorce.

Instead of marriage, Gretchen had begun a loving, long-term relationship with a man she had known since childhood. "Now I can go home when I'm tired of doing what he wants."

Unable to speak up for herself, Kate was programmed to do what her Inner Adult/mother did. Unless we taught her Inner Adult Role Model to be assertive, Kate, like Gretchen, would have to agree with her partner or leave.

Unless we changed the post-hypnotic suggestion, I could almost predict a divorce would occur at about the same time in Kate's life as it did in her mother's. Kate was aware that she was following her Inner Adult Role Model mother's relationship pattern, from selection to solution, and wanted Psychogenetics to save her marriage.

EXERCISE:

1. Imagine how your parents' relationship (#8) would have been if they had been alike. Think about them both as being like your mother, then both as being like your father.

2. Then imagine that your parents are like another couple that you liked in your childhood. Think about how your childhood programming would have been different with each of these three sets of parents.

3. Write out those new Inner Couple patterns.

9. *Like Father, like Son*

"It's just like looking in a mirror. My Dad is, or should I say *was*, my Inner Adult Role Model. I sure can see my old self in him. I really must have changed though, because I can't stand the way my Dad is with his girl-friend now. He thinks she's having an affair just like I used to think Angela was. He's always accusing her of something. I used to be jealous like that. It's the same thing all over again. I guess I was just doing what came naturally. Dad says his father was also real jealous and possessive with his mother and never wanted her to go anywhere without him. I guess that is where Dad learned it.

"Funny as this is, I'm not jealous anymore since I did those roleplays, but now Angela is. Her father was real jealous of her mother, too, and Angela never liked that in him either. It's that pair bond thing, isn't it? One like this and one like that! Maybe as long as I was being jealous like my father, and hers, Angela didn't have to fill that role in the Inner Couple. She could be like her mother and feel insulted. Now I'm like both our mothers and she's like both our fathers. It's really weird how Inner Couple pair bonds repeat themselves. Truth is, I don't want us to be like any of them anymore. Help!"

EXERCISE:

1. Check back to your grandparents on both sides to find similar couple pair bonds.
2. Look at your siblings' adult couple relationships with their adult partners. Do you find they have one partner like your mother's personality and one like your father's?
3. Check your partners' family, past and present, for pair bonds similar to his or her parents and yours.

10. Like Father, like Daughter

"I'm out of character when I'm with R. J. For some reason I don't understand, he brings out the meanness in me. I'm so critical and grouchy with him. I flip right into it. Just the sound of his voice gets me cranky. It's baffling, because I'm not like that with everyone else. I don't want to be doing this to him. He is so kind to me and would do anything for me. Why does he love me so much? I'm not comfortable being a mean person. I don't even like myself when I'm around him. If I have to choose, I'd rather be with someone who is mean to me. In fact, I usually have been."

Checking Rachel's Selection Test, I could see how similar she and R. J. were to her parents. R. J. brought out Rachel's impatient Inner Adult/father in her.

"Everything my mother did got on my dad's nerves, too. I wondered why he even married her. I know they had a good sex life even though they didn't like to do anything else together. Mother worked at night and Dad worked during the day. They rarely spent any time together. When she'd come home, Dad would fuss at her about her clothes, her hair, her friends, her interests, the way she ate . . . it was awful. They always had money problems and they could never come to any decisions about what to do to fix them. She'd spend money when she got mad at Dad and he'd close her charge accounts. They went bankrupt twice. It was always a crisis," Rachel told me, shaking her head back and forth. "Strangely enough, I can only be around R. J. a little bit at a time or he starts to bother me, too. I don't know why he puts up with me."

I can guess . . . his mother and father had an Inner Couple pattern similar to Rachel's. R. J.'s Selection Test bore out my hunch.

"My Mother and Father were always going in opposite

directions," he wrote. "Mom usually went places without my father and vice-versa."

Rachel laughed. "I'm usually attracted to guys who are not interested in me. R. J. was different, I guess, because I wasn't interested in him when I first met him. But he was so persistent about dating me, I finally gave in just to see what it would be like. Now I can't stand it . . . all his gooey-gooey stuff makes me so uncomfortable. I want him to chill . . . leave me alone. But he's about to give up on me. And I don't want him to go away."

Rachel seriously wanted to change her pattern. Now she realized that her Inner Couple blueprint led her to either be in love with someone who was ignoring her, or to ignore someone who was in love with her.

"What's it like to have both people in love at the same time?" Rachel asked me.

Well, of course, mutual affection would be unfamiliar to her. I didn't think she could tolerate it without some Psychogenetic reprogramming first. Right now, Rachel's pair bond pattern required that only one partner in the couple be loving, never two. This is one of the typical programmed interactional binds that occurs with couples. A set of ineffective cues and responses can keep their relationship out of balance, but in familiar conflict.

Rachel had a lot of homework to do. To start, I had her rewrite several of the scenes she remembered from her parents' life together so that she could practice having an Inner Couple who enjoyed being together. Several times, we roleplayed her opposite parents working together on the money issues instead of against each other. Gradually, Rachel became less oppositional in her own relationship with R. J. and learned to cooperate as a part of a couple instead of staying stuck in her parents' historic couple conflict.

11. How Nice Guys Can Finish First

Martin and Connie came to see me after Martin had been arrested for driving while intoxicated. I saw them separately to hear each side of the story. Martin began:

"It's weird that this would happen to me. I don't even know why I started drinking. My first wife Tiffany was an alcoholic. She didn't drink when I met her, but after we got married, she started big time. Never again, I vowed, would I ever be around anyone who drank like that," he said emphatically.

"So, for my second wife, I picked Connie, a quiet, respectable gal who had never gone into a bar in her life. So what happened? Would you believe it? I started drinking myself. The truth is, Connie is so even tempered and agreeable, I'm bored to tears around her. I jokingly tell my buddies, she drives me to drink, but it's not funny anymore. The sad truth is, I miss Tiffany. She was wild and crazy but I liked the excitement around her. We'd go to bars and meet all sorts of interesting people. The same bars Connie has to drag me out of now. Figure that one out if you can!"

Switching roles didn't make any sense to Martin at first, but after the Selection Test, it did. By the end of the first session, he understood why his first wife had left him.

"I bored her, didn't I?"

Yep.

"Tiffany used to say I was such a stick in the mud, always wanting to stay home on the computer and never go anywhere. When I heard myself calling Connie a stick in the mud, I started to wonder what was happening with me and that's when I decided I had to come see you."

By the next session, Martin was aware that he was in a Psychogenetic trance. His mother was an alcoholic.

Not coincidentally, his father was, in his mother's own words, a stick in the mud. Martin's father was his Inner Adult in the first relationship, with Tiffany, but his mother was his Inner Adult in the second relationship with Connie. In effect, Martin switched from behaving like his mother to behaving like his father when he picked Connie as his second mate. So both marriages ended up the same. In each, one partner drank in bars and one stayed at home. Martin wanted to be like neither one now.

"Can I break the spell, go back to the way I was and stay with Connie, too?" he pleaded.

We invited Connie in so I could hear her side of their history. Connie was excited that Martin had actually been to see me twice already.

"My mother was a heavy drinker. I grew up listening to my father plead with her to stop drinking," she said. "I met Martin after I swore off alcoholics forever."

Even before her Selection Test, I could have predicted that Connie's mother would be her Inner Mate Model, because Connie had consistently picked men who drank, as her mother had . . . until Martin came along.

"I liked Martin because he had been married to an alcoholic before and we both swore we'd stay away from drinkers altogether. We had a lot in common when we were dating. But after we got married, Martin changed for some reason I could never understand. Last month, for the first time, I heard myself yelling the very same things to Martin that I'd grown up hearing my father yell to my mother: 'Get off the booze!' I swear I stopped in my tracks. It was a *deja-vu* experience. How did I ever get into my father's role?"

I explained the Psychogenetic theory of programmed mate selection to Connie and invited her to take the Selection Test.

"Now I have hope Martin can go back to being the man I fell in love with when I first met him," she said.

They began the process together. Two months later, they had a real breakthrough. Connie came in beaming.

"Well," she said, "I remembered when we roleplayed what we wanted our parents to do, so right before Martin was getting ready to go out again, I went over to him and gave him a big hug instead of yelling at him. He started crying and told me he didn't know why he'd acted so cold to me when I was everything he had ever wanted in a wife. We went in the kitchen and had a long talk. It was like our personalities switched back right then and there to how we were when we first met. We both want to stay out of trance. I think that Selection Test made it easy for us to see that what we were doing with each other hadn't worked for our parents. It didn't make sense to keep doing it."

The Selection Test also made it easy for them to see their matching Inner Couple sets, each with a drunk and a homebody. Opposites. Two drunks or two home-bodies might not have had such a problem with each other. The Psychogenetic exercises aimed at rebalanc-ing Connie and Martin so they could utilize the pluses of both Adult Role Models on the Selection Test and redesign the minuses. Reprogramming started by having Martin and Connie roleplay their parents being nice to each other at the same time, in order to increase Connie and Martin's tolerance of simultaneous affection between themselves. They needed to practice having their parents find fun without alcohol and excitement without trouble.

"Martin has always wanted to sail," Connie told me on their final visit. "We're writing a make-believe story about our parents being friends back when we were kids and having a sailboat together. We're remembering how much we enjoyed growing up together and crewing during the summer," she said.

Martin agreed. "I like thinking that Connie and I have known each other that long. Our parents are planning a month together in the Caribbean and that'll happen as soon as we write the next chapter. We are having more fun pretending we grew up together."

I'm reminded of the words of author Tom Robbins, who ended his popular novel, *Still Life With Woodpecker*, with this thought: "It's never too late to have a happy childhood."

ONCE UPON A TIME EXERCISE

1. Make up a childhood experience about you and your partner growing up together as friends and falling in love with each other. It will be easier to reprogram yourself if you write it down.
2. Imagine you became childhood sweethearts and had similar "plus" parents and friends

VIII. THE RESULTS

Many ideas grow better when transplanted into another mind than in the one where they sprang up.

—Oliver Wendell Holmes, Jr.

1. In-Laws or Outlaws

When I was young, I was a typical little girl in that my father was the man of my dreams and my mother was my gender role model. I wanted to grow up and be a mommy like her and marry a daddy like him. I had always loved my father dearly. Early on, he gave me a sense of freedom and independence. As a child, most of the conflicts I experienced were with my mother. She and I looked alike and according to the current theories, I would grow up to be like her, too. My quiet, intellectual father was much more easy-going and trusting of me.

My loving but stricter mother was very protective and, in her own words, harder on me for my own good. Since adolescence, I wanted to both make my mother proud of me and get away from her control. When it came to boyfriends, my mother was outspoken in her opinion. She thought my childhood boyfriend was too quiet and moody and didn't pay enough attention to me. It skipped my notice until much later that she had the same complaint about my father not having enough time for her. As a teenager, I was already somewhat confused between her admonitions to marry someone who would take good care of me and my own longing for my first love who, in my mother's words, had left me all alone while he went away to college. "If he's ignoring you now . . ." my mother would say, warning me of less

208

attention to come from him in the future.

As much as I loved my father as a father, for some reason by the time I was eighteen I had changed and didn't want to marry a man like him—a real dilemma, since my childhood sweetheart was like my beloved father in many ways. Even though we had drifted apart and I had started dating someone else, it wasn't until I met my new boyfriend's family that I considered marrying him. My boyfriend and his father looked a lot alike. My future father-in-law and I liked each other from the very first meeting. For some reason I didn't understand, I also felt right at home that night with my new boyfriend's mother. My mother also loved my new, attentive boyfriend and encouraged our budding relationship.

After our marriage, it became more and more obvious my husband wasn't turning out like his father. In fact, he hadn't ever been close to his father, who was my favorite in-law. My husband's favorite parent was his mother and he was very much like her in disposition. She was much too controlling for a daughter-in-law like me, who had spent her teenage years wanting to become independent from her own mother. How had I not realized my husband was more like his mother . . . and mine? Both he and my mother complained I didn't make enough time for them. Both my mother and my husband thought I was much too independent for my own good. For a long time I believed that and tried to simultaneously please and break free of both of them.

As the years went by, the association between the three of them became more identifiable. My husband and his mother usually agreed on how to handle a situation, and my mother idolized my husband and usually took his side in any disagreements he and I had. He wanted me to be more like my mother, and his. My father-in-law and I had similar opinions on things, as did my father and I, and after my own father died, my

father-in-law stepped in and became an alternate father
to me. We became fast friends, as were my mother and
my husband. I used to laugh and think to myself how
mismatched both my parents and my husband's parents
had been. Both sets were opposites. It got me to wondering why opposites attract, marry, and stay together,
arguing as they do. Not that I was the first human to
ever ask such a question and have it go unanswered.

Hundreds of books have been written on the subject
of mate selection. The common belief when I married
was that the father was the little girl's Mate Model and
the mother, the little boy's. As the popular old song said,
"I want a girl just like the girl who married dear old
Dad." In our case, my husband had to deal with the
growing realization that he had married a girl just like
dear ole Dad, not Mom. As millions of other newlyweds
before us discovered, people don't really know each
other until they marry. Rarely do they realize ahead of
time that one of the potential in-laws they meet will
show up inside their future mate. To most of us, in-law
trouble has always meant outside interference from one
of the partner's parents. We've all heard mother-in-law
jokes, but few newlyweds complain about the father-in-
law, when actually the interference can come from
either.

Psychogenetic theory states that the real problem
many couples encounter is not external interference
from in-laws, but internal interference from programming that begins to surface inside each partner after
they become a couple. In effect, the prior example of
your parents' relationship is *trance*-ferred into yours. It
is not your Inner Child that picks your mate. **That
theory exists simply because your Inner Child
grows up and makes the same mating decision as
your programmed Adult Role Model parent did.**

The Inner Adult contains the mating energy that
Freud called the libido, or the sex drive. That is the part

of your personality that drives you to be attracted to a certain type of person, to select that mate to marry and have children. It explains who really introduced you to your mate. In every sense of the word, it was truly a blind date. In the trance of falling in love, you do not see the person in front of you, you see the original Mate Model parent, someone who reminds you of the other half of your Inner Couple, whether that person looks like that parent or not. **While your conscious mind is looking for the perfect mate for your future, your subconscious mind is searching for the perfect match to your past. And your subconscious mind *is* in charge of what you get. You get a person who can act like your Mate Model parent.**

Now, years later, I realize the Inner Adult/father part of my personality picked someone for me like my Inner Mate mother and my ex-husband's Inner Adult/mother part picked someone for him like his Inner Mate/father. My father, his father, and I were all alike, as were his mother, my mother, and him. Both of these sets of parents were opposites, as were we. Both his and my Inner Couple sets contained one like this parent and one like that parent and the interactions between them were the same.

Bingo! . . . We were a perfect match. Together, we provided each other with another opportunity to work through our previous generation's unresolved couple issues. But under stress, we slid right back into our parents' old patterns. Like them, we could not solve the riddle because we got stuck in trying to change each other instead of *trance-forming* ourselves and our own Inner Couples, in that order.

2. From Generation to Generation

I began to see with my own marriage, as with the couples who came to my office for counseling, that our **learned relationship behavior automatically brought us right back into our parents' melodramas and left us there with the same ineffective solutions they had.** As impressionable children, each of us were hypnotized by watching and listening to our Adult Role Models. They, in turn, had been hypnotized by theirs, and so on backwards through the generations. Researchers have debated whether it is environment or heredity that determines how you will be as an adult. Is the glass half full or half empty? The answer is *both.*

The premise of Psychogenetics is that you inherited one parent's personality through your genes; from birth to five years of age you subconsciously copied the behavioral and interactional style of that parent; and then as an adult you searched for someone to fill the other adult role. In that way, your early environment preconditioned how you would be when you grew up. The example of your Adult Role Model in an adult relationship was demonstrated over and over to you as an impressionable child and formed your Inner Adult programming.

You are programmed from childhood to act, react, and interact as one of your parents did then in his or her adult-adult relationship. You picked a mate who could respond the way your other parent did then. Your post-hypnotic suggestion is to recreate what happened between them when you become part of a couple. We would all prefer to think that the problems we have in our relationships are caused by our partner's behavior and have nothing to do with our own participation. The truth, however, is that the difficulty we have comes from inside us not from our partner. The cause of our unsolved couple problems is hidden in our parents' relationship and the effect shows up in ours.

Their Inner Couple example is the post-hypnotic suggestion—not known to our conscious mind, but all too known to our subconscious. Unless we work on the Inner Couple parental imprint level, we cannot effect permanent change in our own couple system. True healing begins when we come out of trance and first recognize that Inner Adult imprint in ourselves. Waking up means that we realize that some of the *trance*-gressions in our relationships are our Inner Couple *trance*-ferences coming from our own early programming. That's the problem, not the solution. **The solution lies not in what our partner should do to fix the relationship, but in the knowledge of what our Inner Couple role models could have done to fix theirs.**

Until we become trance-*parent*, and see our parents as the two people they really were, we cannot interrupt our own post-hypnotic suggestions. Instead we will remain expert judges of our partners' behavior and stay quite blind to our own imprinted patterns. The Selection Test acts as a wake-up call. Sooner or later, in order to change our relationship pattern, we must all come to terms with our own imprinted parents and fix our own Inner Adult and Inner Mate. Until this happens, we will not be free to seek another type of mate or relationship. The first order of unfinished business here is to change our imprinted memory of our *own* parents' couple behavior, not our partners'. Unless we work first on our own Inner Adult imprints, we cannot effect permanent change in our current interactional system.

We are not asking our partners for improvement in their external behavior. We are instead restructuring our own internal cues and responses. Psychogenetics heals from the inside of each partner first. We cannot change either our outside behavior or our partner's until we become aware of our own imprinted Inner Couple.

Psychogenetics seeks to have each of us first change that imprinted pattern of cues and responses by creating a false memory, only in this case, it is a positive interactional experience that we are adding, not a negative one. The original ineffective Inner Couple imprints are still there, only now we have one or more other options. It is of paramount importance that we experience these positive Inner Couple precedents through roleplay. Otherwise, we won't be able to interact in a new way under stress.

Even if you did manage to send a new cue, or receive a new response from your partner, unless you have an internal precedent, you might not recognize or believe the new response. "That can't be real," you might say, or "She doesn't mean it." If there is no positive Inner Couple precedent in your subconscious, your old negative self-fulfilling prophecy will respond for you. Your Inner Adult will proceed to bring back that old familiar parent's interactional behavior, simply because that is the only end result possible in a couple relationship for you, according to your imprints to date.

For years, we've known that negative couple interactional patterns repeat themselves. This was clearly shown with the alcoholic and the enabler, where it was seen over and over again that the alcoholic stopped drinking but the enabler continued to enable the now sober partner until the familiar drinking behavior returned. Just like water seeks its own level, couple interactions seek their own family environment. In order for permanent change to occur, the original family memories must change.

We describe these family-of-origin imprints as self-fulfilling prophecies, when they are really parent-fulfilling. In any case, they are only self-

fulfilling if we had positive role models for relationships. **Negative post-hypnotic suggestions are most unfulfilling.** Through the various Psychogenetic exercises, each of you now has an opportunity to do what you wanted your Inner Adult Role Model to do back then, and recreate that parent's new behavior with your current mate, here and now.

3. Second Chance

The Selection Test that you filled out in the beginning of this book was a map through your early childhood programming and a checklist to reprogram your "minus" (–) Inner Adult and Inner Mate Models. Take a look at the minuses on that test. They identify the sections that you need to reimagine, rewrite, roleplay, and re-solve in your parents' history so you can reenact them on your own.

Repeating the healing exercises in this book can reprogram you and your current mate to interact with each other in ways that you wanted your parents to do. Each time you roleplay a scene from your parent's relationship in your childhood, you are creating a new alternate solution for that particular issue. One by one you can *re-solve* them all and practice these new solutions yourself.

I quote from an article by Renee Emunah entitled "Drama is Therapy," which appeared in the April 1993 newsletter of the California Institute of Integral Studies. The article explains in well-stated terms the effect that roleplaying one's parents as you wish they had been can have on one's belief systems and corresponding behaviors.

> In life we are subject to patterns of behavior, habitual response. We fall prey to restrictive self perceptions and the influence of others' limited expectations of us. In the world of make believe, these constrictions do not apply. We have the freedom and permission to do what seems to be so difficult to achieve in life; to alter behavioral and role patterns under the guise of play and pretend we can for once act in new ways. The bit of distance afforded by drama enables us to gain perspective on real

life roles and patterns and actions and to actively experiment with alternatives. Drama liberates us from confinement. Whether that confinement is socially or psychologically induced, the dramatic moment is one of emancipation.

4. Reimagining a Happy Ending

It was once a practice of mine to ask couples to write their parents' real childhood histories, who they were as adolescents, teenagers, young adults—the story of how these parents met, and what they were like when they first married. Of course, all of that was hearsay, but clients still brought in many a family story from their childhood and anecdotes from the lives of their parents that were useful to me in finding generational patterns.

Now the first homework assignment I give them, if possible, is to actually interview their parents. I ask them to bring their parents' taped or written accounts of their own life histories to our sessions so we can get information from their parents' childhood all the way through the clients' childhood. I've often invited client parents in to give their histories themselves. Often they told me confidential details they had never told their children. I began to notice, however, that the parents' secrets were very similar to my clients' fictional versions in our roleplaying exercises. Until then I hadn't realized that the three-chair roleplaying exercise actually accessed subconscious Inner Couple files each time we did it. I had told my clients to just make up a story when they told me they didn't know anything about their parents' relationship before they were born.

However, my clients' early relationship histories and their parents' relationships during their early childhood years was also similar. Over and over again, the parents' histories consistently matched the problems we were working on at that same stage in my clients' lives. I could not explain the coincidence, but I knew it was a generational pattern. Actually, I was realizing that these problems had been in their families a lot longer then we had thought, and that my clients needed somehow to be reprogrammed so that these patterns wouldn't be endlessly repeated.

Now instead of just roleplaying their parents' past and fixing it, I also ask my clients to write their parents' future . . . and make it happy! Sound preposterous? Do it anyway, I say. The very act of imagining how good it might be for your parents as a couple will create an alternate goal inside of you for your own childhood and begin to change your imprinted Inner Couple script. The positive new interactional pattern will work its way into your memory bank whether you believe it is possible or not while you are writing it. You will still have access to your original Inner Couple memories, but now you will have other, more positive experiences from which to choose. You will have taken your first step towards fixing your own relationships by experiencing how things could be if your parents lived happily ever after.

Make sure the new scenarios you wish for your parents are in the present tense, as if you are that Adult Role Model parent as you write them ("I am my mother at twenty years old and I have just met the man I will marry. . . ."), and then write them in the past tense as you retell that parent's happy history with his or her mate ("When my mother was twenty years old, she . . .").

Use the actual people and events, only change the outcome so that the situation ends as happily as you can imagine it for them/you. Then do the same for your other parent. One or two pages for each parent will do. You might find speaking the new stories out loud into a tape recorder helpful after you've written them. You can play it over and over again. Frequent listening will speed up your Inner Couple reprogramming.

EXERCISE:

1. Rewrite your parents' mating years, from their teens to when they met each other—falling in love, getting married, getting pregnant.)

2. Bring their happy relationship up to the point where they are expectant parents for the first time, and then all the way to when you are born. Write about how happy they were during the first five and ten years of your life, how their relationship got better over the years.

3. How would you feel if that happened with you and your partner now?

5. Wish Fulfillment Exercise

By doing the following wish fulfillment exercises, you can change your Inner Couple and bring the improvements forward into the now. By reenacting a variety of positive changes over and over again, you can have an effect on which patterns will be handed down from your parents' generation to your children's generation through you.

PART I: Set up three empty chairs in a triangle, one for your Inner Child, one for your Inner Adult, and one for your Inner Mate. Do not worry if you cannot remember anything about how your parents were with each other. Start anyhow. Do not worry if you do not consciously recall much about these two people. Their personalities and behaviors will easily come back to you once you start to roleplay. If not, let your intuition be your guide. Rely on stories you heard about them. Most of the time, that will access the feeling memory or the insight you need.

1. Sit in one of the chairs and introduce yourself as your Inner Adult parent. Speak in the first person present tense, as if you were that parent as the adult person he or she was back then, in your childhood. As that parent, say out loud how you feel about yourself and your mate. Example: "I am my mother Eunice. I am thirty-seven years old and my daughter Anne is nine. My husband Eddie is a good man but works too hard and is too tired to spend much time with me when he gets home."

2. Move to the other chair and introduce yourself as your Inner Mate, and proceed to do the same as above. "I'm Eddie and my wife Eunice thinks I'm not affectionate enough. But it's just I'm so busy. . . ."

3. Return to the chair of your Inner Adult Role Model parent and imagine the other parent sitting across

from you. Say the same things to this Inner Mate Model parent that you heard your Inner Adult parent say to him or her when you were a child.

4. Sit in the Inner Mate parent's chair. Imagine yourself as this Inner Mate parent and respond by saying the same things that he or she might have said to your Inner Adult Role Model parent when you were a child.

5. Sit in the Inner Child chair. Imagine yourself as a child watching their interaction as it was, remembering what you wished your parents would do.

6. Remember which parent you wanted to do something first to fix their problems. Sit again in that parent's chair and interact with the other parent the way you, as a child, would have liked him or her to have interacted.

7. Sit in the other parent's chair and respond the way you would have liked that parent to have responded.

8. Go back and forth as much as needed until you are satisfied that your parents have solved their recurrent problem in a new way. Let them express their withheld feelings, positive or negative, to each other until they become caring towards each other, no matter how long it takes or how many tries are required. Persist until they have a solution. Do not stop until you have imagined a way that works for them. Then roleplay that positive, new interaction. Write it down and read it out loud over and over again.

9. Repeat this process with any other negative Inner Couple memories you want to change; in fact, the more times you repeat it, the better the results.

NOTE: If you are single, stop here. You can practice these exercises once or twice a day. You are evolving your Inner Adult's history and your self-fulfilling prophecy. What will begin to happen is that your subconscious mind will be reprogrammed to seek out a similarly evolved and more satisfying Inner Mate for yourself. Your *new* Inner Adult will be reprogrammed to interact with that *new* Inner Mate more as your Inner Child *wished* your parents could have interacted with each other. Your *new* Inner Couple will automatically reflect your *new* memory of your parents' new positive relationship, instead of their *old* one. Go to Part III.

PART II: These steps are for your mate to do with you.

10. First have your mate take the test and also do Steps #1-9 alone.
11. Look on this Childhood History Chart to see how your parents' personalities and interactional behaviors match those of your mate's parents and see the similarities in the two Inner Couples.
12. With your current mate, roleplay both your new, evolved parents, each of you taking the role of the parent you are most like. Roleplay your Inner Adult parent while your partner plays your Inner Mate, unless, of course, your new solution has produced two Inner Adults and two Inner Mates who are alike, then you could play either one.
13. Then redo step #12 as above with the two of you roleplaying your partner's parents.
14. Each of you write your parents' new relationship histories and tell them to each other out loud.
15. Could you be that way with each other, too? You may want to start with "Once upon a time" and end with "lived happily ever after."

Part III: For singles or couples, on the next page fill in a third Selection Test. This time write it the way you wish things had been in your childhood.

2. Describe the looks, personality, and behavior of your mother (or female parent) as the adult person you wanted her to be when you were a child (0-10 years old):

Ideal

Step One: Childhood

8. Describe parents' relationship with each other when you were a child (0-10 years old) the way you wished they were then:

6. Ideal Mother-Child Relationship:

4. Describe mother as the parent you wanted her to be when you were a child:

1. Describe yourself as the child you could have been if home life was ideal (0-10 years of age):

Selection Test™
History Chart

3. Describe the looks, personality, and behavior of your father (or male parent) as the adult person you wanted him to be when you were a child (0-10 years old):

7. Ideal Father-Child Relationship:

5. Describe father as the parent you wanted him to be when you were a child:

6. The Perfect Mate

Alice was smiling as she walked in. I hadn't talked to her for three months. During that time I had been working with Irving, her ex-husband, whom she had started seeing again.

"Irv has improved a hundred and ten percent," she said. "He isn't demanding anymore and he doesn't always have to have his own way all the time. He's still a little uptight but my dad's uptight, too, so I know what to expect there. Actually, Irv's close to perfect now. No jealousy. No pouting. The only thing is that he's still nervous that I might end up hooked on prescription drugs like his mother. I can't even have one aspirin without him looking twenty years into the future and projecting his fears that I'll be stumbling around the kitchen every night like she does. He's not fussy about it, just scared.

"But things are so much better with us since Irv started Psychogenetics with you. I have something now that I've never had in a relationship before with any of my other boyfriends—a man who's my best friend. I really like Irv now and I trust him. He's dependable and consistent. It's not just a mad passion thing between us anymore. We're talking about getting remarried now."

Alice was an only child. In fact, she was the only child of an only child.

"I've always liked my time alone and now Irv is finally willing to let me have more of that. I didn't grow up around a lot of people and I still prefer to be by myself. When we were married the first time, Irv crowded me too much. He was always wanting more time and having to know where I was going whenever I went somewhere. I like this better.

"My mother and father were in their late thirties before they married and each one had established their own independence before they met. I like that model. My mother had plenty of resentment about having to do so much around the house after she got married. Her advice to me was to not start babying a man because I wouldn't like giving up my free time once he got used to it and started demanding I keep it up. She wishes she hadn't ever babied my father. But I just couldn't say no to Irv if he needed something done, and then I'd end up resenting him. That's why I left."

I gave Alice some homework. I wanted her to have some additional behavioral options in her Inner Adult programming, so I asked her to write two new memories of her mother. The first new memory she imagined was her mother not agreeing to do things she'd resent later. The second was her mother agreeing to do things for her father and not resenting them. These new precedents were important because right now, Alice was stuck in either-or, all-or-nothing behavior.

Conditioned by her Inner Adult/mother to say yes and resent it, or say no and feel guilty, Alice had no-win solutions behind both Door Number One and Door Number Two. I wanted Door Number Three and Door Number Four to be guilt-free *wins,* which is exactly what Alice also wanted in her relationship with Irv.

We roleplayed her two new scenarios during the next session and implanted these new options into her subconscious.

"I'm even going to write in a time when my mother did an errand for my father in exchange for him going to the symphony with her, which is something she always wished he would do."

Bingo! There was Door Number Five!

Talking about opening new possibilities reminds me of Yvette's story:

Yvette was a thirty-two-year-old divorcee who had just gotten a new job that paid twice as much as she had ever made before.

"It's amazing to me not only that this opportunity came to me, but that I was actually able to take it. I don't think I would have even applied for this position if you hadn't had me rewrite my mother's history. There was something to that after all.

I had asked Yvette to imagine a story about her mother going to the top of her profession. Now as she listened, I began a guided fantasy for her. It had all the ingredients that Yvette wanted in her life now.

"See your mother dressed in the very best clothes and imagine her taking you out to lunch at one of the best restaurants in town for your eighth birthday. Listen to your mother tell you about her wedding plans to the man of her dreams. You will be in her wedding. This is a man you will like a lot and he will be a great new father to you. Remember? And you already know at eight years old that when you grow up and get married, your wonderful stepfather will be there to walk you up the aisle and the great relationship you will have is because your mother changed her life way back then."

Yvette smiled. "Just picturing my mother as a successful young woman instead of a dependent, battered wife actually has opened some closed doors inside me that I would never have been able to go through if she hadn't first. I have never before felt worthwhile enough to deserve good jobs or good men. Maybe it is because my mother stayed with my no-good father all his life and never dated after that. Now I feel I deserve a better relationship, too. I've always looked for the perfect mate and never found him. Now I think I could be a perfect mate myself when he shows up. Give me some more homework. I'm ready."

And she was.

7. *Like Father No More*

Tim came in to show me the wedding pictures from Seattle.

"I still remember to this day what happened when you asked me if I was going to make the same decision my father had made, or if I would make a different choice and take another path. I was involved with two different women at that time three years ago. One was just like my Type C mother. Cold, critical, cruel, crazy, and controlling. I had gotten into relationship after relationship with women like that.

"After three months in therapy, and doing all those roleplays and letters and homework, I finally met a new kind of gal, but she seemed much too good for me. I was already so beaten down back then, I wasn't yet sure I deserved to be with someone who had her act together. I didn't think I could live up to that kind of a gal. I felt naturally more drawn to the girl who had a lot of emotional problems. That way, I could feel helpful to her and better than someone if I was with her. If I was with the new gal, I might be the one that needed help and she would be better than I was. I remember all those guided fantasies you took me on until I could get to the point where I could myself imagine good things happening to me," Tim said.

"It was a terrible dilemma. But when you asked if I was going to take the same path in my life that my co-dependent father had, I knew picking an emotionally troubled girl was the same decision my father had made years ago. As a result, he spent his life taking care of and catering to my demanding mother. I bet he wished he had married another kind of partner, who could both give and take, instead of just take and not give anything back like my mother did. It took courage to do something different than my father had. I felt disloyal to him when I didn't follow his role modeling, but my sacrificing my life just to honor his sacrificing his didn't make a bit of sense. I think he would have wanted me to learn from his mistake, so I chose Patricia instead of Lilly.

"I want you to know that my making that dramatically different decision served me well and still does. Patricia and I were married two years ago and are even happier the second year than we were the first. It is the most amazing relationship. She cares for me in a way I have never felt from any woman. Certainly my mother was never anything like her with me or my father. The more I realized how like my father I was, the more I realized I had chosen the same type of mates he had.

"Then I knew that for the first time in my life, I had to choose another type of partner, someone unlike my mother. I'm so glad I did. Patricia is like me. Actually, Patricia and I are both like my loving father—we are exactly the same loving way with each other—the way he always was with my mother. We're 'alikes.' My mother was a harsh, demanding woman, and even as a child I could not stand to be around her. Now I don't have to be around anyone who is anything like her in order to have a relationship with a mate."

Tim's story demonstrates the re-solution of the conflict between his Inner Adult's programming to be like his role model father and remain loyal to his mate, and his Inner Child's need to get away from his mother. In previous relationships, Tim, like his Inner Adult father, had picked women like his mother. On a subconscious level, he had no other choice other than the one his father had made years before Tim was ever born.

The choice of Patricia freed Tim from his negative Inner Couple directive to have one partner like his mother and one like his father, and opened the door for Tim to have his Inner Adult and his Inner Mate be alike in a relationship with Patricia.

"For the first time, I understand why I've always

picked opposites before. I had to. My God, my father was so loving and my mother was so mean. I was stuck in that pattern. I couldn't ever pick loving women because if I was around them, I had to act mean like my mother was and, worse yet, I never knew why. All I knew was nice women scared me, and I felt mad and got away from them fast. If this is what happens when the Cycle of Abuse repeats itself, I can sure see how it does.

"Perhaps now my kids will have a Cycle of Happiness to repeat instead."

EXERCISE:

I. Write down ten positive and ten negative traits of your current or last partner. Give examples to describe that partner's interaction with you. Describe the most prominent emotional feelings between you and this mate.

2. Look back at your first and second Selection Tests. Do some of the characteristics of this current or last partner resemble your Inner Mate parent or stepparent when you were a child or teenager? Write them in that section of the test.

3. Could that parent have had these characteristics and you not known it as a child?

4. Might it explain more about that parent as an adult person?

5. Look at your description of your Inner Adult parent or stepparent as an adult person.

6. Which of your Inner Adult parent's negative characteristics do you not want to find in yourself?

7. Which of your positive traits now might your Inner Adult parent also have had then? Write them in the Inner Adult section of the Selection Test.

8. Does this give you any new insights into who your parents were as people then?

8. *My Mother Herself*

Caroline, a forty-year-old client, said, "When I looked back over my first Selection Test and realized I was more like my mother than my father, I thought I was lost and gone forever. As I roleplayed her, I realized she wasn't so bad after all. She had such low self-esteem. So do I. But I had only listed negative traits for her on the Selection Test, so I went back and wrote in some positive traits for my mother and me, both. Now I wonder how she would have been if she had ever felt good about herself. Things would have been really different.

"You know, I never really knew either of my parents as people. Parents didn't share a lot of who they were in those days. But they went directly into my subconscious mind anyhow, didn't they? I didn't realize how little I knew about my own mother until I started roleplaying her. Then it was as if the whole storehouse of feelings opened up and I could understand her from the inside as an adult human being instead of just my mother. Amazingly, when I looked back at my Selection Test, I didn't have any descriptions of who she was as an *adult* person, only who she was as a *parent*. I realized I had written her from my child's view of her as a parent, not as a person."

A new concept, *trance-parent-see,* came to mind as Caroline was telling me this. Indeed, she had to *see* her *parent* as an *adult* before she could come out of her *trance*. Until that happens, she couldn't differentiate between who her mother was as a person and her mother's behaviors in her parent role.

"That, of course, is the exact problem I've had with my mother," Caroline commented. "I may never have known who my mother was either, until I roleplayed her myself. Then I realized what she went through being married to my father. I'm not angry at her anymore. I don't know if I could have done all the things I wanted her to do with him if I'd been his wife back then. I'm still working on me doing them with my husband and it's a full time job. I actually have a new-found respect for all she did do."

Remember, unless you first understand what is happening on your subconscious parental imprint level and bring your Inner Adult self out of trance, you cannot effect any change in your current couple's system. Roleplaying increases your internal awareness of both parents. For interpersonal change to occur in your relationship now, at least one of you must first create a different space inside, as Werner Erhard used to say. In order for this to happen, we must first prepare a positive emotional precedent so something positive can happen . . . again. In the roleplaying of your parents, you have such an opportunity to do what you wanted your Inner Adult Role Model parents to do back then. With roleplay, you can practice that wish fulfillment behavior with your Inner Mate partner, and through reenactment bring those positive changes forward into the now for yourself.

9. Breaking Up Is Too Easy to Do

Ernest was a young accountant who came in with his wife for separation counseling. I saw him by himself to get some background information.

"Janice still wants a relationship with me, but I don't want to be with her anymore. Nothing I can say to her will convince her it's over between us. What's a guy to do? It was just the opposite with Fran and me. Then I was the one who wouldn't let go. I kept calling Fran long after she started dating someone else. She wouldn't return my phone calls, but I wouldn't give up. I started to stalk her. It was awful. I was glad I wasn't on that side of the equation this time. I feel guilty that I'm hurting Janice that much, but it's better her than me. I'll stick around long enough to ease out gracefully. What else can I do? One of us is going to have to leave town."

Ernest's Selection Test gave me some vital information about his couple belief system right away. His mother was his Inner Adult Role Model. Both of her marriages had been short-term relationships. Ernest's father left her when Ernest was two years old. As to her second husband—you guessed it—she left him when Ernest was only five. Fran, Ernest's first wife, was like his father and Janice, his second wife, was like his stepfather. Both of these men were Inner Mate Models in Ernest's early years because they were in a primary relationship with his mother, and therefore had an effect on his pair-bonding programming. Unless we could evolve Ernest's Inner Couple programming, he would continue to leave or be left. In each of his following relationships, Ernest would be on one side or the other of this Inner Couple program, unless he changed that imprinted edict now.

First, I asked him to write happy endings to each of

his mother's marriages, and then we roleplayed those scenarios. As a result of this and several other reimagining exercises, Ernest developed an alternative option that allowed him to stay with Janice. For the first time in his memory, he had two precedents for staying, instead of only two precedents for leaving. Roleplaying his mother and her partners working their problems out with each other implanted the idea of a solution instead of a breakup. We had now created the possibility for something positive to happen with Ernest by having something positive happen to his Inner Adult Role Model.

Three months later, sure enough, he and Janice took off on a second honeymoon.

"It's a miracle," he wrote on the postcard from Cancun. "This time we both left, only it was together for a change. We're falling in love all over again."

Since I developed my theory of Psychogenetics, I no longer have clients deal first with their troubled relationship with their current partner. Instead, I ask them to deal first with the ineffective communication patterns they inherited from their parents. As the motion picture *Field of Dreams* points out, "If you build it, they will come." We simply remember the old setting and let the clients build a new, untroubled Inner Couple pattern over it.

The first Selection Test you filled out helps you locate which of your parents' troubled patterns you are still using. The roleplaying of your parents as they were helps you to understand each of your parents' unmet relationship needs from the inside of their personalities and behaviors. Roleplaying your parents as you wanted them to be provides an opportunity for you to experience them meeting each other's needs for a change. Having new memories of your parents *re*-solving the emotional conflict between them produces enormous internal satisfaction for your Inner Child, too. The new solution gives you the long-awaited completion of their unfinished business and an alternate positive program for your relationship now. What if it had really been that way in your childhood?

10. They Lived Happily Ever After

Example #1: Client after client had already changed his or her selection pattern using the Psychogenetic System. With tears of joy in her eyes, Jan told me how grateful she was that someone had finally come up with a system to explain to her why she kept getting involved with the wrong type of guys—up to now. Six months later, she was married to the kind of man that she thought she would never meet, much less marry.

Example #2: "Rita is just like her mother," David said. It was only a compliment because now Rita liked her mother. Until now, comments such as this would have started a fight in their house. In the early days of their relationship, David had said that very thing to hurt Rita. But since Rita roleplayed her mother and developed an understanding of who she was as a person, Rita was actually proud to be like the new, improved Adult Role Model.

"I wish my mother could have had the same kind of couple counseling I had. Then she could have felt better about herself and maybe my father would have, too."

What Rita wanted her parents to do differently may have been the same as what her parents wanted their parents to do differently. As a result of roleplaying, Rita finally got to see her mother change her pattern. As a result, Rita's own patterns changed automatically.

Example #3: Betty was thinking about having another baby. Looking radiantly beautiful, her green eyes sparkling, she came back a year later to tell me how happy she and Nolan were with each other now.

"It's unbelievable that just two years ago, I was thinking about leaving Nolan for Ralph. I must have been out of my mind. Nolan and I have been so happy ever since I realized the ghost of my father was active inside me.

It all makes so much sense now. I feel so happy now. I actually understand for the first time in my life why I was the way I was, and it has given me such peace of mind to have conscious control over my behaviors. I am not compelled to be like my father anymore. He and I are at peace with each other. Nolan and I are, too. Now we are living as we want our kids to do when they grow up."

Example #4: "I almost didn't know how to act with these new people. They are so affectionate with each other." Yvette said. "They all sat on the sofa, close to each other. My new boyfriend's mother and father were affectionate with each other. They called each other pet names. They were warm and accepting to me, too. It was so different from my family. Actually, it was just like I had roleplayed—just the way I wanted my mother and stepfather to be with each other. And here were Tony's parents doing it in front of me. I've never had a birthday party like that before in my whole life. I went home after that and my real mom and dad were arguing like they usually do. My father was in his room with the door locked. Mother was in the kitchen crying. I swear, it made me remember all the times I wished they had divorced when I was a kid. I like the made-up memories I have of Mom and her new husband better every day. Tony's parents really are like that. That's how I want Tony and me to be when we get married. I want us to live the way we would like our kids to live when they grow up."

Example #5: "We're doing well," Natalie reported. "I've implemented the changes I imagined for my parents last year. I feel a lot better since I did it, too. Several people have told me I look better. Gary and I just had another wonderful weekend together. It's like going back to our past when we first met, only knowing each other real well at the same time. I'm liking being with Gary again instead of being afraid of what would happen if I'd ever let myself love him.

"I did what you wanted and asked my parents what broke them up and they gave me two different answers. The truth is they either don't know or don't want to admit their own part in it. After ten years they still want to blame each other rather than look at their own family patterns. I'm glad that didn't happen to Gary and me. Understanding where my parents got stuck and evolving their relationship past that point is what brought us back together. Then we realized how much alike our Inner Couples were."

Example #6: "Our old roles and inherited patterns have changed so much," Sylvia said. "It's like being on a first date again. I haven't felt this excited by anyone in years. Everything is new. I won't even have sex with Mark yet because I have to wait till I know him better. We make out like teenagers though. On Saturday nights, we go to the movies and have long talks at the lakefront. I've gained an understanding of him and for the first time he knows who I really am and how I feel about things. Last time we had sex right away when we first met, because we couldn't talk about feelings. It was an escape mechanism, not love-making, but we didn't know the difference then."

Mark agreed. "Sex was just a release of tension for me. Now I really feel love for Sylvia. I like this new woman who is also the mother of my children. We're equal partners in raising our children. What's gone from inside both of us is the anger our parents carried around for each other all their lives. Now we can relate without that underlying tension being repeated in our tonality, impatience, and distance."

IX. THE SOLUTION

What if space shifted and time bent and we could meet ourselves as we'll be twenty years from now? What if we could talk face to face with the people we were in the past, with the people we are in parallel lifetimes, in alternate worlds . . . ?

—Richard Bach

Let me conclude with one of my favorite fantasies, one very close to me personally.

I picture my own parents taking turns reading this book out loud to each other. We're all sitting out on the front porch. That's the way our family spent many an evening when I was a child. Mom and Dad are going over some of the anecdotes in *Why We Pick the Mates We Do* and relating them to their own lives. Imagine that! The smell of baked apples is coming from the oven. Together with vanilla ice cream and a cup of my father's special spoon-dripped coffee, tonight will be one of those special family evenings I will always remember. But more than the treat of the coffee for me as a child, is enjoying the special closeness my parents have with each other now.

For the first time, I hear my father talking about his feelings, instead of just keeping them to himself. My mother is smiling and tears come to her eyes.

"I've been wanting us to talk like this again for so long. I remember when we first met. We used to talk for hours. I've missed that, Eddie," she says.

241

"Well, those days are back again to stay, honey," my father replies as he leans over to give my mother a kiss.

I make a note to be more affectionate with my partner, too.

"Let's show Anne how a couple can really be happy together," my mother says.

I love seeing my parents together like this. That kiss is one of the happiest pictures in my memory and I put it there. I always wanted them to live happily ever after and now they are. In my own mind, I have evolved my parents' relationship and begun the process of improving my own Inner Couple programming.

And you can, too. I'm sure of it!

THE END

. . . or could it be the beginning?

If you would like additional copies of this book, the cost is $18, which includes shipping and handling To order Anne's other book, " History Repeats Itself," the cost is $10 each for either the book or audio cassette, which also includes shipping and handling.   You may order either title by calling 1-800-GESTALT or write to her at the address below. Anne would appreciate hearing from her readers.

Anne Teachworth, MA, Director
Gestalt Institute of New Orleans/New York
1539 Metairie Rd. Ste E
Metairie, Louisiana 70005
www.gestalt-institute.com

PRAISE FROM READERS

"I would have never thought there was any way to fix my relationship problems until I read WHY WE PICK THE MATES WE DO. It explained my interactive process in such a clear way that I easily understood where I had been messing up. And best of all, told me how to change it. Before you get in or out of another relationship, take the Selection Test. It will improve your interactional behavior from selection to solution."

V.S.

"I have thanked you and your Selection Test one hundred times a day since I met Philip three years ago. He is indeed everything I ever said I wanted but never could find. And the amazing thing is that if I'd met him a year before I read WHY WE PICK THE MATES WE DO, I might never have known he was the one for me. I would have felt 'not good enough' for him from the beginning and stayed away. What a tragedy to never get to know my soulmate."

L.R.

"Buying WHY WE PICK THE MATES WE DO, has been the best investment I've ever made. I've already doubled my monthly income, stopped hollering at my office staff, and gotten my girlfriend to treat me like a human being, too. All because I realized I was so much like my hated father. I learned to stop wishing he had been nicer and instead changed myself. It was easy as 1-2-3 and all in a few weeks."

G.F.

"After I got my divorce, I used the genealogical chart in WHY WE PICK THE MATES WE DO to interview new boyfriends. My own father was an alcoholic. I didn't want to get married until I was sure I'd found someone who would be a good father to our future children. Now, I use the Psychogenetics System to interview baby sitters, maids and secretaries so I'll know how they will behave under stress with our kids, home, and family business."

P.C.

ABOUT THE AUTHOR

Anne Teachworth, MA, is the Director of the Gestalt Institute of New Orleans, which she founded in 1976. In 1977, she began studying Neurolinguistic Programming with NLP's co-developer, Richard Bandler. For over 20 years, Anne has trained and supervised hundreds of people in the mental health field in the art, theory, skills and ethics of counseling. In addition, she has maintained a private practice in New Orleans for the past 25 years. In 1998, she was certified as a Diplomate of the American Psychotherapy Association.

Anne began teaching flirting classes for singles in 1980. In 1987, she and Richard made an NLP video tape entitled *The Art of Flirtation*. It was Anne's work with singles that led her to further explore attraction and selection patterns, develop Psychogenetics and write WHY WE PICK THE MATES WE DO. She now works with people improving their relationships "from selection to solution." Anne has a chapter, "Three Couples Transformed," in "A Living Legacy to Fritz and Laura Perls," a book of Gestalt case studies published in 1996. Her second book, "History Repeats Itself," was published in 1999 in the United States and Germany.

Specializing in couple counseling, Anne has conducted relationship workshops all over the United States and Europe. Besides New Orleans, she is currently presenting workshops in New York City at The Relationship Center, at the Gestalt Institutes of Santa Cruz and San Francisco, California, and the Institute for Humanistic Psychology in Germany. Her schedule is available by calling 1-800-GESTALT or on-line at www.gestalt-institute.com. If you are interested in scheduling an individual appointment, workshop, or speaking date in your area, please contact her at (504) 828-2267. To be trained and certified as a Psychogenetic Consultant, write to Anne at 1539 Metairie Road, #E, Metairie, Louisiana, 70005, USA.

"There are all kinds of more complicated, expensive and time-consuming therapies out there for couples, but the Psychogenetic method in WHY WE PICK THE MATES WE DO, is the most simple, quick and effective system around. I should know, I tried enough of them over the years."

P.F.

"I always knew there was something more to my reasons for choosing my husband than the unmet needs I had with my mother. I spent too much time and money on therapists for that to still bother me. And besides, if my terrible relationship with my mother had been the real reason I picked the women I did, I would have stopped doing it long before I found Psychogenetics."

T.M.

"This easy little quiz in WHY WE PICK THE MATES WE DO, answered so many complicated questions in my life. It is simply amazing no one has thought of this system a long time ago. The divorce rate would have gone down instead of up. This book saved my marriage.

S.P.

"I always wondered why my ex-husband and I got along so beautifully after we were divorced. I wish I had taken the Selection Test before I did. We could still be married, only we would be happy. We're thinking about getting re-married, actually. I think it will work this time now that I know what the problem really was, and have fixed it - Thanks to WHY WE PICK THE MATES WE DO."

M. C.

"WHY WE PICK THE MATES WE DO is a step by step program that showed me how to get *evolved* in a relationship instead of just *involved* in one. Using Psychogenetics, I solved the problem instead of dissolved the relationship.

B.J.